Elbie Lebrecht has enjoyed baking and cooking since childhood. In response to her daughter becoming diabetic, she evolved a system of cooking without sugar.

Born in London, Elbie Lebrecht has degrees in politics and in librarianship. She teaches cookery courses and runs a private picture library. She lives in London with her husband and three daughters.

D0495572

By the same author

Sugar-Free Cakes and Biscuits
Sugar-Free Desserts, Drinks and Ices

SUGAR-FREE COOKING

Elbie Lebrecht

Thorsons
An Imprint of HarperCollins*Publishers*

Thorsons
An Imprint of HarperCollins*Publishers*
77–85 Fulham Palace Road
Hammersmith, London W6 8JB
1160 Battery Street
San Francisco, California 94111–1213

First published as *Living Without Sugar* by
Grafton Books 1989
Revised edition published by Thorsons 1994
10 9 8 7 6 5 4 3 2 1

A catalogue record for this book
is available from the British Library

ISBN 0 7225 2857 4

Phototypeset by Harper Phototypesetters Limited,
Northampton, England
Printed in Great Britain by
HarperCollinsManufacturing Glasgow

CONTENTS

Acknowledgements *vii*
Introduction *1*

1 Breakfast *27*
2 Breads and Scones *32*
3 Spreads and Toppings *52*
4 Biscuits, Bars and Sweet Nothings *58*
5 Salads *74*
6 Chutneys and Spiced Fruit *79*
7 Pastry, Pies and Tarts *84*
8 Fruit Desserts *112*
9 Cakes *132*
10 Sauces *155*
11 Mousses, Jellies, Creams
   and Ice Cream *160*
12 Children's Parties *183*

Natural Sugar and Fibre in Food *189*
Index *193*

ACKNOWLEDGEMENTS

Jasmine Challis, senior dietitian at University College, London, has validated the carbohydrate and calorie counts in this book, compiled the food table and helped me with accurate nutritional information. I am very grateful for her expert advice and practical experience.

Material from Drs Kenneth Heaton, Erik Millstone and Michael Weitzman helped clarify points that arose in the Introduction. Anne Freeman provided constructive editorial suggestions. Lorraine and Freddy Isaac and Marion and Nigel Scott volunteered to test and taste some of the recipes. Yonatan Kahn was a valuable judge of sweetness levels.

My husband has been a source of counsel and concern and, with my girls, Naama, Abigail and Gabriella, played an essential role in the creation of this book.

INTRODUCTION

This book defines the dangers of sugar, examines its invasion into our way of life, and demonstrates how each of us can live a full, vigorous, enjoyable life without it – and without even missing it.

Sugar is not – contrary to what the producers want you to believe – a daily necessity. In fact, it is not necessary at all in your diet, but if you have become used to the taste, you will want to be weaned off it gently.

Your decision to start giving up sugar will have an eventual bonus – the gradual adjustment of your taste-buds to the natural sweetness in the foods you eat. At the end of the first year without sugar I suddenly noticed that sweet corn really was sweet, and so were onions and carrots. When the cake that used to make your life complete tastes cloyingly sugary you will know that your taste-buds have begun to sort out the natural sweetness from the chemical.

Finding alternatives can be a slow process. A couple of women students in my cookery class complained of suffering from terrible sugar cravings, finding themselves getting up in the middle of the night, raiding cupboards for sugar or chocolate. I consulted two doctors on their behalf: they both diagnosed a hormonal or metabolic imbalance, disagreeing sharply about its causes, but both prescribing treatment of a high-fibre diet of wholewheat bread, jacket potatoes, plenty of fruit and vegetables and no sugar or white flour.

Eating healthily is pointless if it makes you feel awful. A regime that forbids cakes and sweets quickly becomes oppressive and encourages the feeling that the forbidden food is the most attractive. Sweet treats are part of our culture and it is difficult to sidestep them. The purpose of this book is to provide tempting alternatives which satisfy at the same time as altering perceptions of sweetness. The recipes for cakes are intentionally light rather than the familiar wholefood slabs that sink to the bottom of the stomach. The emphasis is on fibre, but this includes a lot of fruit as well as whole grains.

The balance of recipes in this book is unusual. The bulk of it is devoted to cakes, biscuits, pies and sweets – food that is not an essential part of our diet. The reason for this balance is that the overriding concern is how to enjoy sweet flavours without using sugar.

How to shake off sugar – stage by stage

1. Cut it out of *tea and coffee*. This is often the hardest step and you may only be able to do it after reducing sugar in the rest of your diet. Avoid artificial sweeteners – they will not re-educate your taste-buds to appreciate the taste of natural sugar.

2. Adopt the *cake and biscuit* recipes in this book and adapt your favourite recipes to sugar-free ingredients (see the introductions to Pastry, Pies and Tarts, and Salads).

3. Eat your meals with *fresh fruit* or fruit-based pies and compôtes.

4. If you need *snacks* to keep you ticking over between meals, make sure they are high-fibre ones such as fruit bars, but not laced with honey or any kind of added sugar. Try sunflower seeds sprinkled with soy sauce and baked in the oven until dry, or cooked chickpeas sprinkled with freshly ground black pepper and salt. These make scrumptious bites, are high in energy and very nutritious.

5. For *soft drinks* either buy the apple-based fizzy drinks from health food firms and supermarkets, or make your own with fizzy mineral water and fruit juice.

6. Look out for *sugar-free foods*. They are increasingly available in supermarkets and health foods shops.

Spot the sugars

To avoid sugar when shopping requires all your ingenuity and skill because it is so pervasive in manufactured foods. Sausages, salami, smoked salmon, pickled herrings, soups and mixed savoury spices are usually sugared. There is one teaspoon of sugar in every tablespoon of tomato ketchup. Vegetables, in most manufactured brands, are canned in a solution of water, sugar and salt. Most packaged bread contains dextrose. Many brands of tinned sauces, such as bolognese and curry, contain sugar, as do packets of soup. Sugar is used with these foods not always for its sweetening powers, but as a flavour enhancer, preservative or bulking agent – individual properties which manufacturers could find in other ingredients.

Sugars appear in such a wide range of foods that careful reading of the small print on the packet is essential. The position of an ingredient on the list indicates the amount used in the food. If sugar appears second on the list, as it does with tomato ketchup, then it is the second main ingredient. The word 'sugar' does not always appear on labels, but instead there might be one of the many equivalent chemical compounds known as 'sugars', all of which are highly refined, containing virtually no fibre, vitamins or minerals. Look out for them:

– *Sucrose* is the name given to table sugar and is found in sugar beet and sugar cane. It is made up of the two sugars, glucose and fructose.
– *Glucose* accounts for 15 per cent of the sugar used in manufactured goods – a threefold rise since the 1950s. It occurs naturally in fruits such as grapes. Carbohydrates we eat are broken down by the digestive system into glucose.
– *Dextrose* is a form of glucose.
– *Fructose* is a concentrated fruit sugar. It is found naturally in fruits, vegetables and honey.
– *Glucose syrup* is made from starch.
– *Invert syrup* is made from sucrose and dextrose.
Most words on an ingredients list that end in 'ose' or include the word 'syrup' are a type of sugar.

Beware of manufacturers' sweeping claims. Close inspection of a new brand of 'sugar-free lollipops' revealed that they were made of hydrogenated glucose which, like sugar, is a concentrated sweetener containing no fibre, minerals or vitamins. A random bottle of orange squash picked up in a grocer's shop proclaimed in large letters 'no artificial colour' which is encouraging, but this does not automatically mean it is particularly healthy. The second and third largest ingredients were sugar and glucose syrup, pepped up by a boost of saccharin.

Sugar-free shopping

As public concern has risen about sugar, a number of companies and supermarkets have begun to offer alternatives. These are having to compete with well-established sugar-sweetened manufactured foods; foods which account for two thirds of UK sugar sales.

Confectionery
More *sweets and chocolates* are consumed in Britain than in any other country – 254 grams (9 ounces) worth per person each week. And

only the Swiss eat more chocolate – just 15 grams (½ ounce) more weekly.

The confectionery industry in 1993 sold £4 billion worth of its wares, an increase of £1 billion in only six years. It spent over £90 million on advertising – much of it targeted at children, grooming today's babies as tomorrow's sugar-junkies. The message of TV commercials is reinforced in the sale of sugar and chocolate models of popular figures like Postman Pat and Thomas the Tank Engine. Children under 16 make up one third of all sweet and chocolate consumers, but purchase only one tenth of manufacturing output. In other words most sweets are bought for children by misguided adults.

Successful alternatives to sweets are hard to find – no one has yet worked out how to make bull's-eyes, barley sticks or lemon sherbet without sugar. A sugar-free sweet is a totally different product. Yogurt- or carob-coated raisins, dates and peanuts are the closest manufacturers have got so far. They are produced by a few firms and are most enjoyable. Carob confectionery can be found in health-food shops, but read the ingredients list carefully as 'raw sugar cane' is sometimes used as a sweetener.

Fruit bars can be a minefield for sugar avoiders. Scrutinize the wrappers and you will find that many contain both sugar and honey. Fruit leather strips have a light and pleasant taste although they are pricey. Fig Cakes use fruit, nuts and spices to attain exquisite delicacy. There are combinations of inventive and tasty fruit bars without sugar or honey.

Drinks

Over a quarter of a million tonnes of white sugar was poured into the soft drinks produced in Britain last year – principally cola drinks, lemonade and orange and lemon squashes. Soft drinks consumption has increased more than five times in the last 35 years. The increase in America has been even greater. 'You go to supermarkets and there's just aisle after aisle of junk – avenues 50 feet long with soft drinks on both sides,' warns Michael Jacobson, director of the Washington-based lobby Center for Science in the Public Interest.

The sugar content in a bottle is more heavily concentrated than one would imagine: tonic water contains 3 teaspoons of sugar, an average can of cola contains 7 teaspoons, and Lucozade, which is promoted as an energy-giving drink, contains 8 teaspoons of sugar per glass. Ribena, the popular children's drink, contains 5 teaspoons of sugar per glass. Undiluted, it consists of 60 per cent sugars – the rest is water.

Alternatives can be found in specialist health-food shops and supermarkets. Fizzy drinks with an apple-juice base and a variety of flavourings added are no longer unusual. Expensive but delicious concentrated juices based on apple plus another fruit, such as strawberry or blackcurrant, make a welcome alternative to squashes.

Baby drinks have undergone a dramatic change, with the syrupy liquids which comforted generations being exchanged for concentrated fruit juices. These drinks should still be well diluted. Labels should always be carefully studied as many manufacturers find it hard to shake off old habits of adding glucose, syrup and other sugars, even to new products like herbal teas for babies.

Biscuits
A limited selection of manufactured *biscuits* can be found in the shops. Quality is very mixed, and as with all manufactured goods you have to shop around to find the right brand. Those that have a balanced use of dried fruit seem to get it right. The growth in the numbers of small bakeries in the 1990s has seen some specializing in biscuits that do not use sugar. A bakery chain in North London, M & D Grodzinski, is now producing a range of sugar-free biscuits using recipes I have developed.

Breakfast cereals
Most *breakfast cereals* contain added sugars. Often the name tells you everything – Sugar Puffs or Sugar Smacks are apt descriptions of the product. Others have names that conjure up the healthy life, but still come drenched in sugar. However, those old standbys Puffed Wheat and Shredded Wheat, made from the whole grain, are widely and cheaply available. Sweeten them at home with dried or fresh fruit. Muesli is widely available, but some manufacturers still sweeten with raw cane sugar and honey instead of dried fruit alone.

Yogurt
The typical carton of *fruit yogurt* has two to three teaspoons of sugar in it. Sweeteners range from raw cane sugar to aspartame. The best fruit yogurts are made in a couple of minutes at home with natural yogurt and fresh fruit.

Savouries, jams and fruit
Sugar-free *baked beans*, *curries*, *chutneys*, *relishes* and *mayonnaise* are found in health food shops and supermarkets.

Sugar-free *jams* or *fruit spreads* proliferate. Whole Earth and Meridian are the leaders with a vast choice of flavours.

Crunchy and smooth *peanut butters* are made with sea salt and no sugar by a small number of food firms. You will need to experiment to discover the taste and texture that suits you best.

Scrumptious carob spreads – usually a mixture of ground hazelnuts, peanuts and carob powder sweetened with apple juice – are made by health-food firms.

Tinned fruit in natural juice is made by many of the large supermarkets' 'own brands' and by the well-known tinned fruit manufacturers.

Baby foods

When it comes to *baby foods*, careful reading of all ingredients is essential. Not all jars of savoury baby food are without sugar, and the dried versions in packets usually include sucrose (sugar) and maltodextrin (glucose syrup). One firm's version of cauliflower cheese has maltodextrin as the second ingredient, even before the cauliflower. Fruit desserts are invariably sweetened with sugar. Rusks remain high in sugar. Even the low-sugar version contains only one gram less than the regular rusks, and it still contains more sugar than a digestive biscuits.

The combination baby cereals contain a mixture of sucrose, dextrose and fructose, but plain baby cereals such as Porridge Oats and Protein Baby Cereal can be sweetened at home with fruit.

Natural sweeteners

Our taste-buds enable us to savour and enjoy a sweet taste and there seems no reason to deny this pleasure. Sugar should not be its source. The main sweeteners used in the recipes in this book are dried fruit and fresh fruit. The great advantage of using fruit is that it comes packed with vitamins and minerals – a sure way to avoid the alarming recent incidence of scurvy reported among teenage girls whose diet consisted mainly of cola drinks, chocolate, hamburgers and crisps.

Dried fruit – prunes and dried apricots need some soaking before using, but dates, figs, raisins and sultanas, once washed and rinsed, can be chopped or boiled with water to make a mushy paste. If the recipe requires a smooth paste, blend after the dried fruit has absorbed all the cooking water.

Fresh fruit – banana and apples are the most commonly used. Either mash peeled bananas or if they are to be used in a swiss roll-type sponge put them through a food mill or a sieve to make a smooth thick liquid. Use apples with the peel if possible, but always wash well first.

Depending on the recipe apples can be grated, sliced or puréed with a little water in a blender.

Juice is only used in small amounts in the recipes. This is because when drunk by itself it can raise blood sugar levels rapidly because it is liquid and contains no fibre. Juice offers nutritional benefit by providing vitamins and minerals, and for the best flavour there is nothing better than freshly squeezed juice.

Artificial sweeteners

Artificial sweeteners only prolong the dependency on unhealthy, oversweet food. Research studies and reports have linked artificial sweeteners with serious health problems and this excludes them from being a viable alternative to sugar.

The most popular sweeteners are saccharin and aspartame.

Saccharin – my daughter returned home from a party with a packet of American chewing gum in her party bag bearing the slogan, 'Use of this product may be hazardous to your health. This product contains saccharin, which has been determined to cause cancer in laboratory animals' – a nice going home present, I thought.

This warning is the result of a compromise by the USA Food and Drugs Administration which had announced a proposal to ban saccharin from all processed foods, soft drinks and as a table-top sweetener in April 1977. This decision followed research studies which showed that saccharin caused bladder cancer and had led to its total banning in Canada.

Recent research indicates that rats fed saccharin eat 15–20 per cent more food than normal. This confounds the implicit sales message that it provides a way of avoiding extra calories.

Saccharin is extensively used in Britain in such products as soft drinks and pickles, and in products marketed as low calorie or diabetic. Food Regulations specify that it may not be used in baby foods.

Aspartame is sometimes sold under the name of NutraSweet or Canderel. At the beginning of 1984 it was used in only four products but is now widely used in soft fizzy drinks, soft drink concentrates, slimmers' yogurts and desserts.

Permission for its use in fizzy soft drinks in the USA was only granted by the Food and Drugs Administration in 1983. Millstone and Abraham argue in *Additives, a Guide for Everyone* that 'we cannot be certain that the tests to which Aspartame has been subjected are adequate, even by the relatively poor standards of current best practice, and so we cannot be confident that Aspartame is safe.'

There are restrictions on its use in Austria, Belgium, Greece, Italy, Holland and Portugal. The UK government has issued warnings about its use by sufferers from phenylketonuria who require a diet low in phenylalanine.*

Sorbitol is used in ice cream, confectionery, chewing gum and soft drinks. It has been used for a long time in foods intended for diabetics. Large doses produce diarrhoea, although in children small doses have a similar effect. When my daughter, a diabetic, first went to infants' school the kind-hearted cook used to make special sugar-free versions of crumbles and pies for her. She loved them. It took me a little while before I linked this with her doubling up over the toilet when returning home.

There is also some evidence that high doses contribute to the formation of bladder tumours.

Honey

Honey is made by bees, as everyone knows. The bees remove a dilute solution of sugar from plants and concentrate it, resulting in a substance that is 76.4 per cent sugar.

Honey has never been eaten as a basic food, but always used sparingly. Nature made it so difficult to obtain that we must assume it was never intended for large-scale consumption. This particular sweetener came with a sting. King Solomon warned, 'It is not good to eat much honey' (Proverbs 25,27). Honey is not as concentrated as sugar, but like it contains no fibre and very few nutrients; consequently it is not used in my recipes.

Although many people extol the virtues of honey and mistakenly describe food made with it as sugar-free, it contains no B vitamins or any other vitamins. It has very small amounts of minerals, including some trace minerals.

How to dry fruit

Fruit is traditionally dried out in the sun, but if you don't live in a hot country you can dry fruit by other methods. An ordinary oven, used in a slightly different way from usual, can dry small quantities of fruit,

*Phenylketonuria is an inborn defect of protein metabolism causing an excess of the amino acid phenylalanine in the blood which damages the nervous system and leads to severe mental retardation.

while specially designed food driers are sold in some kitchen shops, although they tend to be expensive.

Dried fruit is readily available from supermarkets or can be bought in bulk from specialist outlets or wholefood warehouses, so there is rarely any need to dry fruit unless you have a glut of fruit or your freezer has broken down. Apples, apricots, bananas, cherries, grapes, plums, pears, figs, pineapple and strawberries are all suitable for drying. Fruit used should be ripe, fresh and unblemished.

Drying is an effective method of preserving fruit because the food is made inhospitable to bacteria and moulds by removing much of the

---

Minerals and dried fruit

Dried fruit is high in minerals. Compare the figures below for dried fruits with those for sugar, glucose and honey.

(tr=trace, – = unknown)	Sodium	Potassium	Calcium	Magnesium	Phosphorus	Iron	Copper	Zinc
Sugar	tr	2	2	tr	tr	tr	0.02	—
Glucose	150	3	8	2	11	0.5	0.09	—
Honey	11	51	5	2	17	0.4	0.05	—
Dried apricots	56	1880	92	65	120	4.1	0.27	0.2
Dried dates	5	750	68	59	64	1.6	0.21	0.3
Dried figs	87	1010	280	92	92	4.2	0.24	0.9
Prunes	12	860	38	27	83	2.9	0.16	—
Raisins	52	860	61	42	33	1.6	0.24	0.1
Sultanas	53	860	52	35	95	1.8	0.35	0.1

(McCance and Widdowson, The Composition of Foods, 1979)

---

water. It is a slow process, and the fruit is reduced to 20–25 per cent of its original weight, darkening and taking on a wrinkled appearance.

The basic procedure is to wash the fruit and remove cores, stalks, stones and pips. When cutting the fruit, slice it into even-sized pieces so that each piece will require the same amount of drying. Fruit can be laid straight on to trays or first dipped into boiling water or steamed to crack the skins. Discoloration is avoided by painting the fruit with lemon juice or a solution of ascorbic acid (vitamin C) and water.

The trays used should be made of wood or stainless steel mesh with sufficient space for the air to circulate. The fruit is laid out evenly without any overlap. Halves of fruits such as peaches and pears are placed skin side down which prevents the fruit from sticking and speeds up the drying time by exposing more of the cut surface of the fruit.

The fruit is dried in a food drier at a very low temperature – gas mark ¼/70°C/200°F. The amount of drying time depends on the size of the fruit. Allow 6 hours for apple slices, 10–12 hours for halved apricots; 8 hours for halved bananas, 6–8 hours for sultana grapes and 10 hours for plums. Rotate the trays to allow even exposure to the heat.

An oven can also be used for drying small quantities of fruit. When using an oven make sure the bottom tray is at least 20cm (8in) away from the heat source. Do not crowd in too many trays of fruit because this will affect how well it all dries. Switch on to gas mark ¼/70°C/200°F, and keep the oven slightly propped open during most of the drying time.

Test a few pieces of fruit from each tray before removing from the heat. If the fruit is not dried thoroughly it will become mouldy. The aim is to produce dried fruit that is leathery but not stiff. If it is too dry, the temperature of the oven was too high for too long and you will need to allow more time at a lower heat. If the fruit is too hard it means the initial temperature was too high.

Fruit leathers are made by puréeing fruit, spreading it thinly over a tray and leaving it to dry very slowly at an extremely low temperature, even switching off the oven for some of the time. After 24 hours it should be dry enough to peel off. A basic recipe is to combine apple with another fruit.

A freak summer with uninterrupted hot weather may encourage you to try drying fruit outside in the sun. Here are a few tips:

– Use trays which allow a free flow of air.
– Do not leave the trays outside when the weather is sticky and humid.
– Protect the drying fruit from the birds; a net of some kind is one solution.
– Move the fruit around to ensure even drying.

Inside or out, drying is an ancient method of preserving fruit and even if you do not intend to become an expert it is fun to experiment at least once and to observe how the water slowly dries off from the fruit, completely changing its texture and shape.

Storing dried fruits, nuts and grains

Buy dried fruit, nuts and grains in medium-sized quantities unless you intend to use them within two months. If stored for too long they can become stale and lose their flavour. Nuts tend to turn rancid because of their high oil content, so when buying them in a supermarket check the sell-by date. When sold loose, make sure they do not look as if they have spent a long time in the shop. If in doubt do not purchase too great a quantity at one time.

All of these foods can become infested by insects. Infestation is an unpleasant surprise, but it can happen to anyone and does not reflect on the cleanliness or tidiness of your kitchen. One way to prevent or at least contain an outbreak is to store food in glass or plastic containers with very tight-fitting lids. Resist monster-size bargain packets which may end up languishing on your shelves and create ideal conditions for a holiday home for maggots.

The flour moth is one of the most common villains. Its larvae can eat their way through whole grains, usually leaving a trail of silken threads. The thin white threads or webbing sometimes found around the outside and inside of packets of oats and flour indicate infestation.

Dried fruits are not too badly at risk. Raisins and prunes are usually insect free. Dates are prone to infestation, but as they are generally fumigated before export any insects or larvae tend to be killed off, but watch out for figs, dried bananas and dried apricots. Infestation experts consider that oil around the fruit can increase the chances of attracting insects because of the presence of extra moisture. Sun-dried fruit is available, but cross-infestation can take place at any stage of the fruit's journey to your kitchen.

Horror stories abound of maggots found in barley, dried apricots, spaghetti, crackers and shelled peanuts bought from health food shops and mass supermarket chains. If you are unfortunate enough to have purchased food in this condition, take it back to the shop and insist on a refund.

Be forewarned and store medium amounts of these foods in jars in cool dark cupboards.

Pesticides and their effects on food

If you are health-conscious enough to consider using whole grains and whole foods, then pesticide residues in your food will be a matter for concern. Pesticides were originally used to help farmers make a reliable living from their crops, but they have proliferated enormously in the last forty years.

The Food Commission, an independent consumer watchdog based in London, claims certain pesticides are linked to cancer, reproductive problems, birth defects and allergic reactions. DDT is an insecticide banned in the UK in 1984 but the residues are so persistent that they enter the food cycle and are still found in milk and meat products. Banned pesticides are sold in third world countries and return to Britain via imported food. Derek Cooper of Radio 4's *Food Programme* wrote about 'Mediterranean countries where lettuces and courgettes destined for British shops are grown in polythene tunnels exposed to a constant mist spray of fertilizers, pesticides and fungicides.'

Organic food is not widely or cheaply enough available to provide a solution. As much of the food we buy has been treated with pesticides here are some ways of trying to keep levels low in your diet:

– Signs of insect damage or visiting slugs indicate that fresh food has not been too heavily sprayed. If it's good enough for the creepy crawlies then hopefully it will be good enough for you.
– Beware of shiny apples. They don't come off the trees looking like that but have been dipped in a wax solution.
– Cut the fat off meat not just to minimize saturated fats, but because this is where certain types of pesticide concentrate.
– Fruit with thick peels such as citrus fruit, bananas, pineapples, melons and pomegranates protect the flesh of the fruit and minimize the effect of pesticides. If you need orange or lemon zest remember that traces of pesticide cannot be scrubbed off and you should use the organic variety. Thin-skinned fruits such as apples, pears, grapes and cherries are not protected in this way and at least should always be washed well before eating and sometimes peeled. The problem with removing peel from all fruit and vegetables is that you miss out on much nutritional goodness found under the surface of the fruit skin.

Organic food

Organic food is grown without artificial fertilizers or pesticides. The result is a better taste and a healthy product, recommended not just by health faddists but also by famous chefs like the French brothers, Albert and George Roux. Organic food is not always easy to find and costs more because of the lower yield per acre. Organic fruit and vegetables are sold in specialist health food shops. Safeways has trail-blazed the way for organic produce in supermarkets. Waitrose also sells organic fruit at selected branches. Organic butchers are few and far between and so are organic cheeses.

Many pulses and grains proclaim 'organic' on the label and your only check is the trustworthiness of the wholesaler or the appropriate supervisory body, of which there are a bewildering number:

– *The Soil Association* lays down the most stringent conditions about crop rotation and use of natural manure and employs inspectors to enforce them.
– *Organic Farmers and Growers* have similar basic standards, but allow

the use of Chilean nitrate and are less strict about crop rotation.
– *International Federation of Organic Agriculture Movements* lays
down international standards. This is necessary because the 700
organic farms in Britain do not supply enough to meet demand and
60 per cent of organic fruit and vegetables are imported from abroad.
– *The Farm Verified Organic Information Centre* is a private body
funded by commercial interests which certifies imported organic food.

The Ministry of Agriculture has established a set of minimum
standards instead of several and has set up a UK Registry for Organic
Food Standards (UKROFS). This benefits consumers and trading
standard officers.

A tip for self-catering holidaymakers abroad is that variations on the
words 'biologique' or 'biologisch' aree used to mean organic produce.

How to adapt sweet and sour recipes

Adapting your favourite sweet and sour main dish to a sugar-free one
is not too difficult. Unlike cakes, which need to maintain a delicate
balance, main courses can withstand a fair amount of manipulation.
The point to remember is to add only a little of the alternative sweetener
at a time so that you have a chance to taste the food and decide whether
to add more. Even if you do overdo it and pour in too many raisins or
apple slices, they do not dissolve in water the way sugar does and can
be scooped out with a slotted spoon.

When you use a recipe from your standard cookery book and find
sugar in it:

– If it is a teaspoon or less, ignore it and leave out the sugar: all it does
is enhance flavours and you can do this by adding more flavouring.
– If it specifies 1–2 tbs (1–2oz) then it is needed for sweetening and you
should use a dried or fresh fruit substitute, or juice.

Don't be taken in by the myth of adding a teaspoon of sugar to home-
made tomato sauce. Fresh, sweet tomatoes plus one spoon of tomato
purée for thickness will always give the best results for a basic tomato
sauce.

Recipe ideas for natural sweet and sour flavours are fillets of lamb
stuffed with rice and dried apricots, stir-fried tofu and vegetables in a
sauce made of orange juice and shoyu soy sauce, rice pilav made with
basmati rice, chopped pepper and onion and sweetened with raisins
and almonds.

Sugar and your health

One fifth of what we eat is made up of sugar, a plant extract that gives your body nothing nutritious and can harm your health.

In the past two hundred years, sugar production has increased 400 times from ¼ million tonnes in 1800 to over 100 million tonnes in the 1990s. The average British adult consumes around 37 kilos (82 pounds) of sugar every year. And this figure does not include sugar-based sweeteners such as glucose used in manufactured foods. These bring the total close to 45 kilos (100 pounds) a year – almost 1 kilo (2 pounds) per person per week. Even if sugar were totally harmless these figures would be cause for concern as healthy nutrients in our daily diet are replaced by an alien intruder.

But sugar is not harmless. At the point of entry to your body it interacts with the plaque coating on the teeth to produce an acid that eats into tooth enamel, causing steady damage and intermittent agony. Once inside you, sugar has been identified as one of the main causes of excess weight, of increasing the risk that you will develop heart disease, high blood pressure and diabetes. Links between sugar and gallstone formation and the development of cancer of the bowel have been indicated by recent research.

The root of the problem is that sugar is a highly refined, low-fibre carbohydrate. In the long process of producing sugar, which involves crushing the plant, clarifying the juice, boiling it down and evaporating the water, separating off and removing impurities from the final sugar crystals, 90 per cent of the plant is discarded. The 90 per cent contains whatever fibre, vitamins, minerals, trace elements and proteins nature may have bestowed. All the remaining 10 per cent does is to sweeten; it provides calories and nothing else for the body.

Even the Sugar Bureau, the promotional and political lobby set up by the producers, concedes that 'it is true that refined sugar contains no vitamins, minerals or proteins'. It argues that sugar's function is 'to make foods palatable and help keep our diet varied'. But sugar makes up 20 per cent of the average person's diet – an alarmingly high amount for a mere flavour enhancer.

The complete removal of fibre from sugar results in a very concentrated sweetener called table sugar which is 99.9 per cent sucrose. Fibre slows down the absorption of food. Without it, sugar is absorbed very rapidly and causes a sharp rise in blood sugar levels. Extra insulin is pumped out by the pancreas to bring the sugar level back to normal. The rush of insulin leads to a swing down to low blood sugar. These ups and downs of sugar levels have a direct impact on moods and behaviour.

When sugar is introduced into a nation's diet, certain patterns develop that have been repeated all over the world. As the country becomes wealthier, more sugar is eaten and the traditional staples such as bread, flour and rice decline, and their dietary contributions are gradually eroded. The nation's health suffers with the depletion of minerals, vitamins and fibre.

Tooth decay

Health reports are unanimous in connecting sugar with tooth decay. The risks of sugar consumption were suspected long before the 20th century. In 1598 a German writer, Paul Hentzner, recorded in his journals that Queen Elizabeth I's black teeth were 'a defect the English seem subject to, from their too great use of sugar'. Today 95 per cent of British adults have tooth decay, and £400 million is spent each year on filling over 30 million teeth.

Tooth decay is caused by the bacteria in plaque, the transparent film that collects on teeth, reacting with sugary foods to form acids which dissolve the enamel of the teeth to produce decay.

The more sugar snacks are eaten between meals the greater the likelihood of damage to the teeth. Continual snacking leads to the bacteria multiplying and convering more sugar to acid. Sucrose, or table sugar, 'the arch criminal of dental caries', has been found to have a more detrimental effect than any other sugar.

Despite this overwhelming evidence the Sugar Bureau, the promotional arm of the sugar industry, produced a video for schools claiming that sugar was not the main cause of tooth decay. The British Dental Association urged health and education authorities not to show the film which it described as 'a deliberate attempt to minimize the dangers done to teeth by sugar'.

Societies which have changed from a high fibre diet to a Western style diet high in refined carbohydrates show an increased incidence of dental decay.

A famous instance of the Western diet's attack on teeth occurred on the Atlantic island of Tristan da Cunha when in 1932 a ship brought in sugar, white flour, jam and other processed foods for the first time. Examining the 162 inhabitants the ship's doctor found that 83 per cent were free of tooth decay and no child under five had a bad tooth. Between 1933 and 1937 ten ships docked delivering sugar, white flour and toothbrushes. By 1937 50 per cent of the islanders were afflicted with dental decay, with the rise most marked amongst young children. By 1955, 88 per cent had bad teeth as average sugar consumption reached 900 grams (2 pounds) per person a week.

Some dental researchers consider that refined starches can also cause dental decay, although not to the same degree as sugar. On the other hand high-fibre food, which requires considerable chewing, is thought to stimulate the production of saliva which neutralizes the acid content in the mouth and provides some protection for the teeth.

Obesity

One in two British adults is unhealthily overweight. 'Sugar,' said the *Obesity* report by the Royal College of Physicians, is 'an unnecessary source of energy in a community with such a widespread problem of overweight.'

Several other UK reports over the past fourteen years link obesity with high sugar consumption and in 1986 the British Medical Association, in their report *Diet, Nutrition and Health*, urged a halving of present sugar intake 'in an attempt to avoid obesity'.

Fats – which include butter, oils, margarine and lard – contain more calories than sugar but sweets are more noshable than chips. Even after a large meal most people can manage to squeeze in a little sweet extra. If fat and sugar come mixed together, as they often do, then sugar makes the fat palatable and the calorie load is multiplied.

Overweight people, whether they are slightly or dangerously obese, suffer the same symptoms to varying degrees. High levels of blood pressure and cholesterol and low glucose tolerance – when the body has difficulty handling sugar or glucose in the blood – frequently arrive with obesity. Low glucose tolerance can establish a basis for diabetes and high blood pressure, and high cholesterol levels pave the way to heart disease. There is no such thing as being slightly obese, any more than you can be slightly pregnant.

Heart disease

Heart disease is the number one killer in Britain. It is killing more people than the great plagues of the Middle Ages, according to Dr Michael Scott, consultant cardiologist at Belfast City Hospital. At the turn of the century only two people in every 100,000 died each year of cardiac ailments. Today the figure has rocketed to 243 in England and Wales and 298 in Scotland and Northern Ireland.

'The people who are at risk from heart disease are those who are obese and those who are diabetic. Sugar is clearly associated with both these conditions,' warned Anne Dillon, Director of the Coronary Prevention Group. She was responding to the BNF's 1987 report *Sugar and Syrups* which contested any link between sugar and heart disease. Obesity increases the risk factors. Studies show that as a person's weight increases beyond a certain limit, the long term risk of heart disease grows. The Coronary Prevention Group urges a massive reduction of sugar and fats and an increase in fibre-rich foods.

Doctors estimate that two-thirds of the annual 180,000 deaths from heart conditions could have been avoided by effective prevention campaigns. Where these have taken place there have been marked improvements; for example, in the USA the death rate has plummeted by nearly 50 per cent to 230 per 100,000.

High blood-fat levels, a factor in heart disease, can be raised in men by high sugar consumption. 'In our first experiments with nineteen young men the sugar-rich diet produced an increase in blood triglycerides in all of them after two weeks,' reports Dr John Yudkin, the veteran anti-sugar campaigner, in his book *Pure, White and Deadly*.

There is a suggestion that eating too much sugar depletes the level of chromium in your body. Low chromium is associated with increased hardening of the arteries, which can lead to heart disease, and with an impaired handling of glucose, which can lead to diabetes. Stephen Davies, a nutritional doctor, notes that 'it is interesting that practically all the chromium found in sugar cane is removed in the refining process'. Refined flour also has low levels of chromium compared to wholewheat flour.

Diabetes

Overweight people are more susceptible to non-insulin-dependent diabetes – what used to be known as maturity-onset diabetes – particularly if there is a history of it in the family. Diabetes occurs when insufficient insulin is produced by the pancreas and as a result the sugar level in the blood becomes dangerously high. Diabetics are advised to watch their weight and to stick to a high-fibre diet. Since high fibre is digested more slowly by the body it keeps blood glucose levels at a more stable level.

Diabetes is one of the oldest known diseases, referred to in the *Ebers Papyrus*, an ancient Egyptian text. In this century, however, it has spread more rapidly than ever before. The National Commission on Diabetes in the USA estimated in 1975 that one in five Americans born in that year would develop diabetes if they lived an average 70 years. In Britain and Western Europe 1 to 2 per cent of the population are diabetic. For every case known, there is at least one undiagnosed sufferer. The causes of diabetes have not been isolated, but nutritional elements are believed to play an influential role. During the Second World War, when sugar supplies were severely restricted in Britain and the National Loaf was mandatory, figures for diabetes fell sharply. In the early 1950s when food rationing was gradually removed they were on the rise again and have continued upwards. Whatever causes diabetes, current medical opinion holds that eating an excess of refined foods, including sugar, increases your susceptibility to the disease –

especially if you are already overweight and have an incidence of diabetes in your family.

Gallstones are linked to obesity and to high calorie consumption. 'A low fibre diet may accentuate a tendency to gallstone formation,' states the *Obesity* report of the Royal College of Physicians. Low carbohydrate slimming diets based on eating small amounts of bread and cereal can actively promote gallstones in people who are already overweight.

The *kidneys* in certain groups of people are at risk from sucrose. It is one of the factors that increases the possibility of a certain type of kidney stone called the idiopathic renal stone.

A study of patients at the Royal Bristol Infirmary suffering from *cancer of the large bowel* discovered that they ate 41 per cent more refined sugar than people in a control group. Since the sugars were often eaten with fats, doctors concluded that a combination of excess sugars and fats encouraged a predisposition to this type of cancer.

There are some people who are naturally *sensitive* or allergic to sugar. When they eat it they get a bloated stomach and diarrhoea. Sufferers usually avoid it.

Adults with *Crohn's disease*, a serious dysfunction of the intestine, eat an excess amount of sugar for many years before the symptoms develop. Doctors have been unable to find a mechanism to explain the relevance of this phenomenon.

Spots and pimples are often the result of eating sweets, chocolates, ice cream and cakes. These are all foods that are particularly high in sugar or combinations of sugar and fat and are usually eaten at the expense of fruit and vegetables.

Sugar and white flour together are often indicted for promoting certain conditions. One of these is *hypoglycaemia*, which is the production of too much insulin. Since the brain cells need glucose to function normally this can lead to faintness, hunger, irritability and sudden mood swings. One of the basic approaches in treating this condition is the total exclusion of refined foods and the introduction of complex carbohydrates such as pulses and wholegrains. Alcoholics often suffer from hypoglycaemia.

Diverticular disease is when small inflamed pockets form in the bowel due to chronic constipation and straining. It is a condition that has become more common since the beginning of the century, triggered off by the increasing amounts of refined flour, cereal and sugars in our diet. This unpleasant condition, resulting in abdominal discomfort and pain, is usually relieved by a high-fibre diet.

Excess sugar can affect *mood and behaviour*, especially in children and adolescents. B. F. Feingold found that sugar when eaten together with certain synthetic additives was a cause of hyperactivity. Alexander Schauss, a former American probation officer who studied the effects of diet on his clients, came to the conclusion that diet was the cause of much anti-social behaviour. High on his list of suspect foods was 'excess refined carbohydrate intake'. He found that 'in some institutions, the quantities of these (sugar added) substances is limitless'. American juvenile detention centres which applied his theories to their menus experienced an improvement in inmates' behaviour. A secret reduction of sugar over three months at a US juvenile-delinquents' home resulted in a 45 per cent reduction in anti-social or violent behaviour. But when Stephen Schoenthaler repeated his experiment with a group of female delinquents no change was shown. Similar research is currently taking place in a centre for disturbed adolescents in Durham, in which half are being given a diet free of refined sugar and additives and containing plenty of fibre and the other half are eating the usual diet.

In many individual researches sugar has been blamed for a variety of other conditions: Dr John Yudkin, Emeritus Professor of Nutrition at London University, links it to breast cancer, enlargement of the liver, the adrenal glands and the kidneys. Dr Stephen Davies, who specializes in nutritional medicine, believes it weakens the ability of white blood cells to fight infection and recommends it should be cut out as part of a package of measures to deal with migraine and thrush. In his latest book Yudkin writes: 'If only a small fraction of what is already known about the effects of sugar were to be revealed in relation to any other material used as a food additive, that material would promptly be banned.'

This section is not meant to read like a catalogue of horrors, but to encourage readers to think more about what they eat and the possible long-term effects. Maimonides, the 12th century philosopher-physician, took the remarkably sensible view that 'no illness which can be treated by diet should be treated by any other means'. Although medical intervention nowadays is less painful and risky than it was then, the principle remains attractive. A slice of wholewheat bread spread with peanut butter is more palatable than swallowing a laxative medicine. Eating fresh fruit salad rather than a chocolate mousse for dessert could save you from becoming a regular visitor to the dentist or to the hospital dietitian.

What you should know about sugar

There is no physiological need for pure sugar. Our body can extract all the sugars it needs from foods such as fruit, vegetables and grains. When refined sugar is eaten it gives a raw burst of energy very shortly after being swallowed. It bypasses the body's elaborate digestive machinery and rushes into the bloodstream, raising the blood sugar level. The automatic response is for the pancreas to produce a lot of insulin to lower the sugar level, but the resulting sudden drop can leave a feeling of tiredness and low spirits.

Concentrated energy can be obtained far more usefully from dried fruits. Sultanas do not explode into the body as sugar does because their concentrated sweetness comes in a complete package with fibre and water and is slowly released into the bloodstream. They contain 250 calories per 100 grams against sugar's 394 calories.

People who participate in sports have no need for sugar. Christine Cross, sports nutritionist for the National Coaching Foundation, considers that a balanced diet for a sportsperson should contain little or no sugar, a lot of carbohydrates and a limited amount of fat. 'Athletes', she says, 'need bread and carbohydrates to build up the energy to train and create muscles.' All sugar does is give sudden artificial bursts of energy, followed by lethargy.

Countless people believe they are helping their own and their family's health by purchasing and using vast amounts of brown sugar of any kind: they might as well be taking four lumps of white in their tea. Fibre is removed from sugar cane at an early stage of refining. Sugar juice is extracted from the crushed canes and is concentrated, crystallized and purified.

Raw cane brown sugar contains some minerals because it has not been purified to the same degree as white sugar. However, the amount of mineral salts it contains is limited, and is about 0.5 per cent. Light brown sugar is usually made from white sugar, often sugar beet, which has been coloured with caramel or molasses. Neither has any fibre. Sugar of any hue has no place in a high-fibre lifestyle.

Sugar has even been compared to a chemical in the basic text *Human Nutrition and Dietetics* (R. Passmore and M. A. Eastwood): 'Table sugar is one of the purest chemicals produced in large quantities by modern industry', declare the authors.

Why we have become so dependent for daily sustenance on a chemical is a matter for historians and sociologists to answer. This book offers an alternative lifestyle in the form of over 150 different recipes using fresh fruit, dried fruit and whole vegetables as alternative sweeteners. Natural sugar is present in all these foods, but it comes as a complete package with all the nutrients intact.

Sugar and society

There is no escaping the way sugar has conditioned the world we live in. Its cultivation was the source of the slave trade causing up to 14 million innocent Africans to be seized and shipped to the Americas.

It remains the staple of several national economies such as Cuba and Haiti, and produces an annual glut that governments are helpless to accommodate. The Caribbean countries and Europe massively overproduce sugar and need to find a market for it. Medical organizations have been pressured to minimize the health risk associated with sugar consumption.

Nevertheless, in the 1990s governments have finally acknowledged the danger and advised people to moderate their intake. The World Health Organization in its report on *Diet, Nutrition and the Prevention of Chronic Diseases* (1990) stated that sugar consumption should range between 0 and 10 per cent of total calorie consumption: in other words half the UK national average, if not less. A document produced by the UK government, *Dietary Reference Values for Food Energy* (1991), stipulated a maximum intake of added sugars at 10 per cent of the average diet – half the amount normally eaten.

Fibre

The great advantage of fibre is that it fills you up and prevents overeating. Foods that contain fibre require a good deal of chewing and the effect of this is to slow down the amount of food you can eat at one go.

Wholefoods and whole grains are beneficial because their fibre and nutrients are intact and not discarded. Fibre in wheat is the wrapping around the kernel which protects the oil, minerals, vitamins, carbohydrates and protein.

Fibre also aids the speedy transit of waste from the body. It absorbs water and swells up to add bulk to the residue food passing through the intestine, hastening its removal. That is why a high-fibre diet, or a bran supplement, is prescribed for constipation. 'Browne bread . . . having much branne . . . fylleth the belly with excrements, and shortly descendeth from the stomacke,' observed Thomas Cogan some four hundred years ago.

Fibre is thought to absorb toxins that can be harmful if they stay in the body for too long, including potentially cancer-forming toxins. Research in Holland shows that diets containing less than 37 grams (1⅓ ounces) of fibre a day are linked with an increased risk of cancer. This may be good news for vegetarians in the West who average 40 grams (1½ ounces) of fibre a day, but worrying for carnivores on 20 grams (¾ ounce) a day. In rural societies in parts of Africa which show virtually none of the common degenerative Western diseases the average daily fibre intake is 70–100 grams (2¾–4 ounces).

How Much Fibre in . . . ?

	amount of fibre per 100 grams (4 ounces)		amount of fibre per 100 grams (4 ounces)
Sugar	0 grams	Prunes	16.1 grams
Glucose	0 grams	Raisins	6.8 grams
Honey	0 grams	Sultanas	7.0 grams
Dried dates	8.7 grams	Bananas	3.4 grams
Dried apricots	24.0 grams	Apples	2.0 grams
Dried figs	18.5 grams	Carrots	2.9 grams

(McCance and Widdowson, *The Composition of Foods*, 1979)

Substitutes

Running out of ingredients is a nuisance, particularly if it happens half-way into making a cake or dessert. Special diets may require omitting a particular food, and certain ingredients are not always popular with everyone. Here is a list of alternatives:

Soya flour – if a pastry recipe contains both wholewheat flour and soya flour it is possible to substitute wholewheat flour for soya flour. The carbohydrate total will increase slightly. Provided the amount specified is very small it can be substituted in cakes as well.

Wholewheat flour – it is harder to find alternatives for wheat flour. Soya flour is not dense enough to substitute for it. Barley, rye and brown rice flour can be substituted, although the results will differ texturally from the original recipe. A number of recipes are included which do not use wheat flour.

Ground almonds – used for their texture-enhancing effect and because of their low carbohydrate count. However, they are expensive even when bought in bulk. An effective alternative in biscuit recipes is finely ground porridge oats. Substitute these for up to a third of the ground almonds and the taste will not be too radically changed, although the carbohydrate content will increase.

Skimmed milk – soya milk is an adequate substitute.

Raisins – can replace dates and vice versa.

Eggs – replace with yogurt or milk in pastry or in a filling requiring one egg.

Butter or margarine – oil can be substituted in cake or crumble-type recipes, but it is not an effective substitute in a rough puff or choux pastry. Pastry recipes using only oil are included in this book.

Sugar-free jams – if you do not have the recommended flavour a similar jam will do.

The recipes included in this book have been made and tested using the listed ingredients so for the best results try and use these.

Freezing

A freezer is useful if you do most of your own cooking and baking. There is not always time or energy to quickly whip up a special cake or extra food for unexpected guests, and if something can be pulled out of the freezer it is very welcome. When you find recipes that you particularly like double the quantities so that half can be frozen.

The basic rules for freezing are:

1. Only freeze food when it is fresh.

2. Food should be cold before being wrapped for the freezer.

3. Always eliminate as much air as possible from the packaging or the food will become dehydrated and flavour, colour and texture will suffer.

Wrap cakes, biscuits and bread in greaseproof-lined sheets of foil in freezer bags or put directly into a freezer container. If you want to keep a watch on carbohydrate and calorie content write a small label with the amount per slice together with the date of freezing.

Thawing

Cakes – keep them in the freezer wrapping while thawing otherwise the cake will lose moisture and the result will be a dried texture.
Biscuits – those with a cake-like texture should be thawed in the same way.
Pastry – remove from wrapping or it will become soft.
Fruit tarts – for the best results freeze the pastry cases and only fill with fruit when you intend to use them, to avoid the pastry becoming soggy.
Bread – keep it in the freezer packaging and thaw at room temperature

for a few hours or so, or leave in the fridge overnight.
Rolls – thaw in the freezer packaging at room temperature for a couple of hours.

Store cakes, biscuits, scones and fruit rolls for up to 3 months. The smaller crisper biscuits are better left for only 2 months. Bread freezes for up to 1 month. Ices freeze for up to 2–4 weeks.

Measurements

Measurements are given throughout in both metric (grams) and imperial (ounces) weights. When the recipes were created metric measurements were used, so if very exact measurements are important to you then it is recommended that you follow the metric set of figures.

Note: the measurements given for bananas are without the peel and those for apple include the peel and core unless otherwise specified.

Basic ingredients

These basic ingredients stored in your cupboards should enable you to attempt most of the recipes in this book.

Brown rice – rice which has not had the outer husk removed, either long grain, short grain or basmati. Available from supermarkets and health food shops.
Butter – butter gives a better taste to pastry, but the question of whether it is more or less healthy than margarine is still hotly disputed. If you choose to use butter, spread it sparingly and make sure that poly-unsaturated oils are also included in your diet.
Carob powder – a dark brown powder ground from the carob pod. Available from health food shops.
Dried fruits – mineral-rich sweeteners and a source of fibre. *Dates* are very sweet and grow in the Middle East and North Africa. *Dried apricots* have their own strong flavour. They are bright orange in colour if they have been preserved with sulphur and dark brown if not. *Prunes* are made from dried plums, and can be bought already stoned. Californian prunes are the best known. *Raisins* are small dried grapes mainly from California, South Africa and Afghanistan. *Sultanas* are made from a special variety of grape originally produced and named after Smyrna in Turkey. They are now grown in Turkey, Greece, Australia, America and South Africa. Sun-dried versions of the last two taste far superior to those preserved in mineral oil. Avoid dried fruit that has been treated with sulphur and mineral oil if you can.

Eggs – free-range eggs are produced by hens that are not housed in batteries. The taste is markedly improved.

Margarine – those high in polyunsaturates and unhydrogenated are recommended. The introduction of hydrogen helps oils solidfy but creates new elements known as trans-fatty acids in the margarine, the effects of which are not sufficiently known. Unhydrogenated margarine is sold by a couple of firms, but it is expensive.

Nuts – almonds, walnuts, hazelnuts and peanuts contain polyunsaturated oils as well as minerals and protein.

Oils – sunflower, safflower, soya bean and sesame seed oil are high in polyunsaturates. Olive oil is high in monounsaturates. Cold-pressed oils are recommended – this is when the oil is not subject to processing at very high temperatures. Avoid oils described as 'vegetable' or 'edible' – they are not necessarily high in polyunsaturates.

Oat bran and germ – these are extracted from the oat grain. Oat bran is high in soluble fibre and is available from health food shops.

Porridge oats – rolled oats, available from grocers, supermarkets and health food shops.

Sesame seeds – small light brown seeds used to decorate pies and biscuits. Available from health food shops.

Soya flour – a pale yellow flour which is high in protein and low in carbohydrates.

Spices – these are invaluable for both sweet and savoury cooking. *Cinnamon* is a dark brown aromatic spice. *Mixed spice* is a mixture of cinnamon, cloves, allspice and nutmeg. *Cayenne pepper* is a hot red peppery spice. *Coriander* is used in Asian and Mexican food.

Tofu – soya bean curd originating from China. It is low in calories and fat and contains proteins and minerals. Available from health food shops and Chinese, Japanese and Malaysian grocers.

Vanilla – natural vanilla essence or vanilla pods are available from health food shops, grocers and supermarkets.

Wheatgerm – the nutritious germ of the wheat. Store in the fridge once it has been opened to avoid it turning rancid.

Wholewheat flour – used as the basic flour. It contains every part of the whole grain – the fibrous husk, germ and starchy endosperm. Available from health food shops, grocers and supermarkets. Finely milled or wholewheat pastry flour is available from specialist health food shops.

Fruit and vegetables

Apples – seasonal eating apples are a handy source of sweetening. Store in a cool dark cupboard or fridge.

Bananas – quite a concentrated sweet fruit. Store in a cool dark cupboard, but not in the fridge as this makes the skins turn black.

Carrots – a sweet vegetable available all year round. Store in a cool dark cupboard.

Oranges – use in season. The segments and juice add a tasty tang to foods. Store in a cool dark cupboard or fridge.

Pears – a very sweet fruit which ripens while stored. Store in a cool dark cupboard or fridge.

Note: All dried fruit, fresh fruit and vegetables should be washed and dried before using, unless, as with bananas, the outer skin is discarded.

1 BREAKFAST

Read o'er this;
And after, this: and then to breakfast with
What appetite you have.
The King in *King Henry VIII*, William Shakespeare

The ideal breakfast differs all over the world. The Japanese start with a bowl of soup while the French get going with black coffee and crusty bread. When I was a student my large, kind landlady would produce massive breakfasts of cereal followed by fried eggs, sausages and potatoes. The other student lodging there would consume all this grease with great gusto urged on by the thought of not having to eat again until the evening. As an impecunious student I was attracted by the economic considerations, but was unable to stomach more than a roll and butter.

Forcing yourself to eat huge quantities of a particular food because a book or parent tells you to is not taking heed of your own needs. Either overdoing it or skimping can result in an unpleasant few hours surmounting the side effects. Individual needs vary tremendously and only you can know what your body requires. The key principle when contemplating breakfast is to decide what you want breakfast to do for you. Is it a brief mouthful, sufficient to give you a little energy until your mid-morning snack, or do you need a meal that will see you through till noon or later? Wholewheat bread or high-fibre cereals provide slow-burning energy, while fruit and juice give an immediate burst. A combination of cereal and fruit will provide a balance of both.

People who simply cannot face food in the morning may manage a bite of toast or a mouthful or two of yogurt or a piece of fruit. For them breakfast is a mid-morning snack or brunch. All the recipes given here can be eaten mid-morning as well as first thing. But do avoid fried food in the morning: it is greasy and heavy on the stomach and represents an assault on a vulnerable digestive system.

A range of manufactured sugar-free breakfast cereals is available, either sweetened with juice or sold as a wholegrain product that you sweeten yourself. Read muesli ingredients carefully – some products confidently declare themselves natural and additive-free but include honey or sugar. If you want to sweeten your porridge try adding a spoon of sultanas or raisins. It means that every flake won't be sugar-coated, but as you are already used to a more natural sweet taste from using the recipes in this book you will discover that porridge has its own enjoyable flavour.

Breads made with wholewheat flour are slow-burning foods, but when combined with a fruit spread (see pages 52–55) or a commercial sugar-free jam they will provide a quick energy boost. Recipes for plain breads, fruit loaf and scones are also included (see pages 32–51). One of the yeast cake recipes with a fruit filling, such as Apple Slice (see page 134–5), also provides a combination start to the day.

This section includes a few suggestions that might be new to you, but why not experiment and try something different?

MUESLI

A walk round the local health food shop will provide a host of ideas for suitable ingredients for home-made muesli. This recipe provides a basic guideline, but preferred grains can be substituted. The grains, particularly the oat bran and germ, will provide a slow-burning meal that will keep you going for a few hours. The dried fruit provides concentrated energy.

75g (3 oz) porridge oats
25g (1 oz) oat bran and germ
75g (3 oz) barley flakes
50g (2 oz) wheat flakes
25g (1 oz) raisins
25g (1 oz) dried apricots
25g (1 oz) brazil nuts

Makes 6 servings

Combine all the ingredients and store in an airtight tin or glass jar.

When serving leave to stand in the milk, soya milk or yogurt for at least 15 minutes before eating. A little grated apple added to the muesli gives a pleasing flavour.

Each serving without milk is 30g CHO. 175 kcals.

FRUIT YOGURT

Dr Douglas Latto, one of the early proponents of the high-fibre diet, has treated serious conditions such as cancer with high-fibre diets. He recommends yogurt and fruit sprinkled with wheatgerm as a healthy start to the day. The fruit provides an energy burst while the live bacteria in the non-pasteurized yogurt help to maintain the balance of bacteria in the intestine.

200g (7 oz) banana, peeled
150g (5 oz) grapes
2 eating apples
300ml (10 fl oz) low-fat
  natural yogurt
2 tbs wheatgerm

Makes 2 servings

Slice the fruit and mix with the yogurt. Sprinkle 1 tbs wheatgerm on top of each bowl of yogurt and fruit.

Each serving is 45g CHO. 250 kcals.

APPLE AND WHEATGERM

A gentle way to eat fruit in the morning is to serve it stewed (see pages 126–8 for instructions for stewing different fruits).

½ recipe stewed apple
2 tbs wheatgerm

Makes 2 servings

Stew the apple according to the instructions (see page 128). Divide it between two bowls. Spoon the wheatgerm evenly over the surface of the apple and either serve as it is or place the bowls under the grill for a few seconds to brown the wheatgerm before serving.

Each serving is 20g CHO. 105 kcals.

ORANGE AND CARROT SOUP

Fruit soups are usually eaten at the end of a meal, but they also provide an invigorating start to the day. This soup should be prepared in the morning. A night in the fridge spoils the taste and excessive exposure to oxygen reduces the vitamin C content of the fruit.

500g (1lb 2 oz) oranges with
   peel
175g (6 oz) carrots
½–1 tsp cinnamon
100ml (4 fl oz) apple juice
100g (4 oz) strawberries

Makes 4 large servings

Peel the oranges and remove the pith. Break into segments and put in a food processor or blender together with the carrots, cinnamon and apple juice to make a thick liquid. If using a blender, first cut the carrots into thin slices. Pour the soup into bowls and garnish with sliced strawberries. If the texture is too thick for your liking add a little spring water to thin.

Each serving is 15g CHO. 60 kcals.

SUMMER PUDDING

This combination of bread and berries provides a light nourishing start to the day.

My daughters, seeing a photograph of this classic English dish in a children's cookery book, were drawn to the violet-purple and red colours and asked me to make it sometime. Towards the end of July, near the finish of the raspberry season, I remembered their request and made this pudding one afternoon as a surprise for the next morning's breakfast.

Redcurrants contain 40mg of vitamin C, and the minerals they contain include calcium, magnesium and iron.

175g (6 oz) wholemeal bread,
  without crusts
250g (9 oz) eating apple
100ml (4 fl oz) apple juice
100ml (4 fl oz) water
250g (9 oz) redcurrants
50g (2 oz) ripe banana,
  peeled
350g (12 oz) raspberries

Makes 6 servings

Cut the bread thinly and put about five slices of bread around the base and sides of a pudding basin.

Slice the apple into a medium-sized saucepan with the apple juice and water. Bring to the boil and simmer until half the liquid has evaporated. Add the redcurrants, having removed their stems, and cook for a few minutes until the juice begins to run and the liquid turns red. Remove from the heat. Strain the fruit so that the juice is separated. Blend the apples, redcurrants and banana in a liquidizer or mouli. Allow to cool a little.

Pour most of the juice over the bread around the sides of the dish, colouring it purple-red. Spoon in half the raspberries. Then spoon half the fruit purée over the raspberries. Repeat this process once more so that there are two layers of raspberries and two layers of purée. Place the remaining slices of bread on the top and cover with the leftover juice. Cover the top of the pudding basin with a plate and put it in the fridge with a weight on top to press it down – a full jar of jam is about right. Leave overnight. Just before serving the pudding, turn out of the dish by loosening the sides with a knife and then inverting it on to a plate.

Each serving is 20g CHO. 85 kcals.

2 BREADS and SCONES

The smell of freshly baked bread is irresistible. Whether it wafts down the street from the bakery or through your home, it is an aroma that goes straight to the senses.

The thought of baking one's own bread is both exciting and daunting. Yeast can be intimidating for many people. If you have grown up with yeast cookery then you are probably free of inhibitions, but if it is a new element in your repertoire, any setback can distract you from ever trying again. I first used yeast at school and remember it as a very unpredictable substance surrounded by instructions about heating equipment and ingredients and fixed temperatures and on and on through a succession of hurdles which grew higher at each jump. The whole business was so daunting that I did not venture to work with yeast again for a number of years.

What changed my attitude was discovering a method of using yeast with no sugar. The mystique dissolved and my anxieties with it, and I became confident enough to handle yeast. The idea of preparing a tray of wholemeal rolls no longer held any fear for me, and a spicy fruit loaf did not intimidate me.

Yeast is a living organism whose activity causes fermentation – a definition only arrived at in 1857 when Louis Pasteur isolated it as a single-celled plant that is only visible under a microscope. The yeast breaks down starch and sugar into alcohol and carbon dioxide. Put in warm, moist surroundings such as damp flour, the yeast responds by setting off the process of fermentation. A natural sugar develops in the dough as it ferments, providing nourishment for the yeast. Although most breadmakers add sugar to their fresh yeast, this is unnecessary, and too much sugar in a recipe at an early stage hinders the yeast fermenting.

The main point to remember when using yeast is not to overheat it before it is baked. Any liquids used should be at body temperature; and when leaving the dough to rise do not put it in contact with direct heat as excess heat will kill the yeast and ruin your recipe.

However, I have found that yeast is resilient enough to non-perfectionists. I do not use a thermometer, for example, to measure the heat of the liquid, but either combine half boiling water with half cold milk from the fridge or dip a finger in to make sure it is no more than body temperature. If the rising stage needs speeding up, put the dough in an oven that has been heated for a few minutes and then switched off, or if you have a spin drier, switch it on for a couple of minutes, switch it off and put the bowl containing the dough inside and close the door. Enclosing warmth is always very effective.

If the yeast cells are kept cold they will remain dormant until placed in a warm damp environment. Fresh yeast can be stored in the coldest part of the fridge for up to 2 weeks loosely wrapped in a polythene bag. It can also be frozen and will keep for 2 months if properly wrapped.

Flour – Wheat is the only grain whose proteins when mixed with water form a gluten strong enough to produce raised bread. The elastic quality of gluten enables the dough to change its shape under pressure and return to its original shape when pressure is removed. If gluten were removed from flour dough and examined it would have a stretchy texture similar to chewing gum. The gluten allows the wheatflour loaf to expand to include the carbon dioxide produced by yeast.

The flour used in all the recipes is wholewheat, containing all the fibre and nutrients of the original grain. A wheat grain is made up of three parts: the outer part is the husk or fibre, which covers the vitamin- and mineral-rich wheatgerm and the starchy endosperm. Plain white flour has had 30 per cent of the grain removed or extracted. It consists largely of the endosperm and contains only 3.4 per cent fibre and greatly reduced amounts of vitamins and minerals.

White bread has always been desired by the rich and cherished as a symbol of purity. The upper classes of Ancient Greece and Rome ate off-white bread which had some of the bran sifted out, and the use of increasingly finer sieves continued into the 18th century. The advent of the steel roller mills in the late 19th century completely changed the methods of production and resulted in flour with a much higher extraction rate.

White bread is still more popular than brown. The British Federation of Bakers estimates that 70 per cent of its present sales are white bread and 30 per cent wholemeal bread. In 1986 there was a sudden 50 per cent increase in the sales of wholemeal bread, but this has steadied as new types of white sliced bread have hit the market. These breads pay lip service to the public demand for fibre by including added bran or a mixture of refined grains, but these are no substitute for the original wholewheat flour.

After baking your own wholemeal bread you will look at shop bread with new eyes. The deep brown hues and light speckled shades of some loaves will suggest the use of caramel or white flour mixed with wheatgerm. Always buy your wholemeal bread from a reliable baker, and if it is wrapped, carefully read the ingredients before purchasing.

Vitamin C and yeast – Fresh yeast combined with vitamin C or, as it is also known, ascorbic acid, speeds up the process of preparing the dough. If you have ever felt intimidated by yeast then this method is liberating because the results are so quick. There are no long anxious hours waiting to see if the bread has risen. When I have taught this method in my cookery classes there is tremendous pleasure and relief at being able to bake a batch of rolls in an evening, and people become receptive to experimenting with new recipes. This is the method used by the commercial bakeries, but tastes and smells rather better when made at home.

A dried yeast already mixed with vitamin C is available from health food shops and instructions for its use are given on the packet. This is worth having in your cupboard for an emergency, but I have found results are best when using fresh yeast.

Basic method of making bread

1. Prepare flour and other ingredients in a large bowl.
2. Pour body temperature (38°C/100°F) liquid over the crumbled yeast and crushed vitamin C tablet and mix into a cream.
3. Pour the liquid and yeast into the flour and bind to make a soft dough.
4. Knead for 10 minutes. This is a very important stage.
5. Cover with cling film and leave to rest for 10 minutes – this is considerably less than the usual 1½–2 hours.
6. Shape the dough and place in a greased baking tin.
7. Cover the tin with cling film and leave to rise for about 40 minutes until the dough has virtually doubled in bulk.
8. Bake in a hot oven.

These are guidelines for the basic approach. Read the instructions for Bread Rolls (see page 35) for a fuller and more detailed account.

BREAD ROLLS

Rolls are even quicker to make than bread because they need less time to rise. With experience you should be able to make and bake these rolls in one hour and ten minutes, and for much of that time the rolls need little attention for they are either rising or baking.

Vitamin C, also known as ascorbic acid, can be obtained from the chemist's. You need ordinary vitamin C tablets, not the fizzy kind. Often it is only possible to buy 50mg tablets, in which case use half.

600g (1lb 5 oz) wholewheat flour
1 heaped tsp sea salt
25g (1 oz) margarine
425–450ml (15–16 fl oz) skimmed milk and water
25g (1 oz) fresh yeast
.25mg tablet of vitamin C
a little milk for glazing

Makes 20 rolls

Pour the flour and salt into a large bowl. Cut up the margarine into the flour and rub it in with your fingertips. (For those who are reluctant to rub margarine into flour an alternative method is to melt it and add it to the flour when it has cooled together with the other liquids.)

Heat the milk and water to body temperature (38°C/100°F). This feels tepid. I find that by combining equal combinations of cold milk with boiling water the temperature is about right.

Crumble the yeast and crush the vitamin C tablet into a medium-sized bowl. Pour some of the warm liquid on top and mix into a cream. Add this liquid to the flour and stir in together with enough of the remaining liquid to make a soft dough. Because you may use less liquid than the amount recommended, or maybe more, depending on the flour that you use, always add the non-yeast liquid gradually.

Remove the soft dough from the bowl and place on to a wooden board or clean work top. Knead it for 10 minutes. There is no one fixed way of kneading bread, but an effective method is to use the heel of your hand to push down on the dough as you fold over the top part. Give the dough a quarter turn and repeat this process. The aim is to achieve a dough that is elastic and supple. If you prefer to use a food processor which has a dough hook attachment for the kneading, look in the instructions for the equivalent machine time of 10 minutes' hand kneading. It is probably about 3 minutes, but check carefully because although it is hard to overwork dough when you are kneading by hand, it can be overworked by a machine.

Return the dough to the mixing bowl and cover the top of the bowl with cling film and a clean tea towel and leave for 10 minutes.

Remove the dough from the bowl and divide it in half. Pat each piece into a long oblong and mark off 10 sections on each one. Break these off and shape them into 20 round rolls. Work them lightly in your hands so that the top side is smooth and any joins are tucked underneath. Place the rolls on a large, greased, warmed baking tray and cover loosely with cling film.

Leave the baking tray in a warm place for the rolls to rise: near but not on the cooker is usually a warm spot. The rolls need a warm environment but not direct heat. After 20 minutes they should have increased in bulk and be ready for baking. Glaze the tops with a little milk.

Bake in a preheated oven gas mark 8/230°C/450°F for 15 minutes until the rolls are browned on top and slightly brown underneath.

Each roll is 20g CHO. 110 kcals.

This recipe can also be used to make a loaf of bread. Instead of a baking tray, grease two 1-pound loaf tins. Divide the dough in half and make each half into an oblong shape, smooth on top with any joins underneath. Cover with cling film and leave to rise in a warm place for about 40 minutes until the dough increases in bulk or reaches the top of the tin. Bake in a preheated oven gas mark 8/230°C/450°F for 30 minutes until well browned. The way to test if it is ready is to tap the underside of the loaf with your knuckle. If the bread has cooked through it will have a hollow sound. If the inside is not set it will sound and feel heavy and dense. Remove the finished loaf from the tin and leave to cool.

Bread Rolls without Vitamin C: *The recipe for bread rolls can be made using yeast alone, without any vitamin C or sugar. The disadvantage to this method is that the dough has to be left longer to rise and a little more preparation is required – the flour and mixing bowl are warmed, a sealed lid is put over the bowl while the dough stands – but it does not have to be kneaded for so long and many bread bakers maintain that it produces a better-tasting roll. The only other difference in ingredients is that slightly less yeast is used – it is reduced from 25g to 20g.*

RYE BREAD

Rye bread is popular in Scandinavia and eastern Europe. Rye flour is low in gluten so when it is used for bread it is mixed with wheat flour which has a higher gluten content, resulting in a loaf with a dense texture. The advantage of a rye loaf is that it stays moist longer than wholewheat bread, and it is quite filling because it takes a long time to digest. This is because its carbohydrates include long chains of sugar units – five per unit. Compare this to glucose which is made up of one sugar unit and is quickly absorbed by the body, or sucrose which is made up of two sugar units.

The caraway seeds used in this recipe give the rye bread a very distinctive flavour, although if you have an aversion to them you can leave them out. Caraway seeds are meant to be good for the digestion and to prevent flatulence.

300g (11 oz) wheat flour
300g (11 oz) rye flour
1 tsp salt
25g (1 oz) margarine
2 tsp caraway seeds plus some
    extra seeds for decoration
    (optional)
350ml (12 fl oz) milk and
    water
25g (1 oz) fresh yeast
25mg tablet vitamin C
50g (2 oz) banana, peeled
a little milk or egg for glazing

Combine the flours and salt together in a large bowl. Rub in the margarine. Stir in the caraway seeds.

Crumble the yeast and crush the vitamin C tablet into a medium-sized bowl. Heat the milk and water to body temperature (38°C/100°F) by combining cold milk with boiling water. Pour this over the yeast and vitamin C and mix in well so that no yeast sticks to the bottom of the bowl. Pour into the flour mixture, stirring the liquid into the flour, together with the mashed banana, and bind to make a soft dough.

Remove the dough from the bowl and place on to a wooden board or clean work top. Knead it by hand for 10 minutes or use the dough hook attachment of a food processor or mixer. Check the machine equivalent of 10 minutes' hand kneading: it is probably about 3 minutes. (See page 36 for advice on kneading.)

Return the dough to the mixing bowl, cover the top of the bowl with cling film and a clean tea towel and leave for 10 minutes.

Remove the dough from the bowl and form it into a long narrow rectangle, folding the ends underneath so that it has a smooth top, and place in a warmed greased loaf tin. Cover loosely with cling film and leave to rise in a warm place for 45 minutes until it has doubled in bulk.

Brush the top lightly with milk or egg and sprinkle over some caraway seeds. Bake in a preheated oven gas mark 8/230°C/450°G for 30 minutes until well browned.

Each 25g slice is 10g CHO. 55 kcals.

BAGELS

These rolls with a hole in the middle are unusual not just because of their shape, but also because they are boiled before they are baked. The result is a very particular taste that is quite delicious so don't be put off by this additional step. In New York bagels are traditionally sandwiched with smoked salmon and cream cheese, while in the Middle East street vendors sell them decorated with hyssop, sesame seeds and salt and they are eaten without any other additions. The wholemeal bagels go very well with any chosen filling; my favourite is avocado.

450g (1lb) wholewheat flour
2 tbs wheatgerm
1 tsp sea salt
1 egg, separated
250ml (9 fl oz) skimmed milk
40g (1½ oz) butter
25g (1 oz) fresh yeast
25mg tablet of vitamin C

Makes 16 bagels

Combine the flour, wheatgerm and salt in a large bowl. Whisk the egg yolk lightly and add to the flour.

Heat the milk and butter in a small pan until the butter has melted and the milk is at body temperature (38°C/100°F). Crumble the yeast and crush the vitamin C tablet into a medium-sized bowl. Pour half the liquid over them and mix to a cream. Add the rest of the liquid. Whisk the egg white stiffly and add to the liquid. Combine with the flours to make a soft dough.

Remove the dough from the bowl and place on a wooden board or clean work top. Knead it by hand for 10 minutes or use the dough hook attachment of a food processor or mixer. Check the machine equivalent of 10 minutes' hand kneading: it is probably about 3 minutes. (See page 36 for advice on kneading.)

Return the dough to the mixing bowl, cover the top of the bowl with cling film and a clean tea towel and leave for 7 minutes. Remove the dough from the bowl, pat it into a long oblong shape and mark off 16 equal slices. Break or slice off and roll each piece into a long sausage about the thickness of your finger. Shape each piece into a ring, carefully sealing the ends by slightly overlapping and working them together to make an even thickness. Leave them to stand on the wooden board or work top for 20 minutes, loosely covered with cling film.

While the rolls are rising fill a wide-based saucepan with about 6cm (2½ in) water and bring it gently to the boil. After the bagels have finished rising, drop three or four at a time into the water. When they have cooked on one side they will rise to the surface of the water. Let them cook for about one minute on each side and use a slotted spoon to turn them over. Remove them from the pan and leave them to drain on a board. Repeat this process with the remaining bagels.

Place the boiled bagels on a greased baking tray. Brush the tops with the beaten egg yolk mixed with a spoonful of water, to give a shiny effect when baked, and sprinkle with sesame seeds.

Bake in a preheated oven gas mark 8/ 230°C/450°F for 15 minutes until they are browned.

Each bagel is 20g CHO. 120 kcals.

FRUIT LOAF

This lightly spiced yeast fruit loaf is baked in a ring mould and tastes delicious spread with creamy butter for tea. A fruit loaf is richer than an ordinary loaf and has a higher natural sugar content. This extra sugar slows down the yeast fermentation so the loaf takes longer to rise.

50g (2 oz) prunes, stoned
50g (2 oz) dried apricots
25g (1 oz) dried dates
300g (11 oz) wholewheat
    flour
50g (2 oz) porridge oats
50g (2 oz) oat germ and bran
1 tsp cinnamon
1 tsp mixed spice
¼ tsp ground cloves
50g (2 oz) margarine
150g (5 oz) banana, peeled
    and mashed
1 egg, lightly beaten
25g (1 oz) yeast
25mg tablet of vitamin C
125–150ml (4½–5 fl oz)
    skimmed milk

Makes 16 large slices

Chop the washed fruit finely. Combine the flour, oats, oat germ and bran and spices in a large bowl. Rub the margarine lightly into the flour. Stir in the chopped dried fruit together with the mashed banana. Mix the egg into the flour and fruit mixture.

Crumble the yeast and crush the vitamin C tablet into a medium-sized bowl. Heat the milk to body temperature (38°C/100°F). Add most of the milk to the yeast and stir well so that no yeast sticks to the bottom of the bowl. Pour into the other ingredients and stir in, adding as much of the remaining warm milk as is necessary to make a soft dough.

Remove the dough from the bowl and place on to a lightly floured wooden board or clean work top. Knead it by hand for 10 minutes, sprinkling more flour on the board if the dough is very sticky, or use the dough hook attachment of a food processor or mixer. Check the machine equivalent of 10 minutes' hand kneading: it is probably about 3 minutes. (See page 36 for advice on kneading.)

Return the dough to the mixing bowl, cover the top of the bowl with cling film and a clean tea towel and leave for 10 minutes.

Remove the dough from the bowl and press into a greased 20cm (8 in) diameter plain ring mould. Cover loosely with cling film and leave to rise in a warm place for 55–60 minutes until it has doubled in bulk or has reached the top of the tin.

Bake in a preheated oven gas mark 7/ 220°C/425°F for 15 minutes. Reduce to gas mark 5/190°C/375°F and cook for a further 15 minutes.

Each slice is 20g CHO. 135 kcals.

DOUGHNUTS

It may seem odd to find doughnuts in the bread section, but doughnuts are basically a rich bread dough filled with something sweet and fried instead of baked. In this recipe they are filled with a stoned prune which bulks them up nicely and means that they cook quickly because the innermost part is not dough. It is also possible to fill them with a jam spread (see Chapter 3) or a commercially made sugar-free jam. Either put the jam in the middle of the dough before frying or cut the doughnut in half afterwards and spread with jam.

24 prunes, stoned, weighing about 200g (7 oz)
450g (1 lb) wholewheat flour
pinch of salt
25g (1 oz) fresh yeast
25mg tablet of vitamin C
300ml (10 fl oz) skimmed milk
50g (2 oz) margarine
2 eggs, size 3, lightly beaten
oil for frying
a little desiccated coconut for decoration

Makes 24 doughnuts

Soak the prunes for at least an hour in a little cold water before using.

Combine the flour and salt. Crumble the yeast and crush the vitamin C tablet into a medium-sized bowl. Heat the milk to body temperature (38°C/100°F) and pour half of it over the yeast and vitamin C. Cut up the margarine and leave it to melt in the remaining half of the milk. Mix the milk and yeast well so that no yeast sticks to the bottom of the bowl and pour into the flour. Stir in with a wooden spoon. Add the melted margarine and milk and stir well. Fold the eggs into the flour mixture to make a dough. If it is a little moist sprinkle with flour.

Remove the dough from the bowl and place on a wooden board or clean work top. Knead it by hand for 10 minutes or use the dough hook attachment of a food processor or mixer. Check the machine equivalent of 10 minutes' hand kneading; it is probably about 3 minutes. (See page 36 for advice on kneading.)

Return the dough to the mixing bowl, cover the top of the bowl with cling film and a clean tea towel and leave for 5 minutes.

Remove the dough from the bowl and break it into quarters. Divide each of these into six pieces. Take each piece of dough and roll it into a ball. Slightly flatten the ball, place a soaked prune in the middle and wrap the dough round it into a ball again. Leave the doughnuts on a board covered with cling film for 20–25 minutes until they have doubled in bulk.

Fill a frying pan with about 2.5cm (1 in) oil and heat until it is sufficiently hot to brown a small piece of bread dropped into the oil. Place a few doughnuts in at a time. Fry for a few minutes until browned and then turn them over to brown the other side.

Remove the doughnuts from the pan with a slotted spoon and leave to drain on absorbent paper. Sprinkle with desiccated coconut before serving.

Each doughnut is 15g CHO. 100 kcals.

SCONES

Scones are quick to make, but there are a few general points to remember:

- *Work quickly so that you avoid overworking the dough*
- *Rub the margarine in lightly so that you get as much air into the mixture as possible*
- *The dough should be softer than pastry which means adding more liquid than you would to pastry*
- *Roll out the dough lightly and pat any leftover pieces out with the palm of your hand rather than rerolling*
- *Scones need a hot oven so always remember to switch the oven on when you start preparing the scone dough*
- *One advantage of scones for fat-watchers is that they do not need to be baked on a greased baking tray.*

Scones achieve their lightness by a combination of bicarbonate of soda with cream of tartar. The bicarbonate of soda is alkaline and the cream of tartar is acid. When mixed with water or milk the alkaline and acid elements enter into a chemical reaction and form a carbon dioxide gas. This gas starts working on the dough straight away. In order to get the full benefit of its raising powers the dough should be put in the oven as soon as it has been cut or shaped.

Mix the bicarbonate of soda and cream of tartar well before adding them to the flour. Baking powder contains the same ingredients already mixed together plus extra ingredients such as wheat flour which prevents the two substances acting on each other before they are needed.

This is a basic scone recipe which combines wheatgerm with wholewheat flour to provide extra vitamins. Wheatgerm is a good source of vitamin E and the B vitamins, and when eaten raw it is said to be beneficial for the digestive and nervous systems. Because of its high oil content it can turn rancid and once a packet is opened it should be stored in the fridge.

150g (5 oz) wholewheat flour
50g (2 oz) wheatgerm
½ tsp bicarbonate of soda
1 tsp cream of tartar
25g (1 oz) margarine
150ml (5 fl oz) skimmed milk

Makes 10 scones

Combine the flour and wheatgerm, bicarbonate of soda and cream of tartar in a medium-sized bowl. Rub in the margarine to make fine crumbs. Bind with the milk to make thick moist crumbs and work these together to form a soft dough.

Remove the dough from the bowl and roll out on a barely floured wooden board or clean work top to a 1.2cm (½ in) thickness. Cut into 10 scones using a 6cm (2½ in) cutter. Place on an ungreased baking tray and bake in a preheated oven gas mark 7/220°C/ 450°F for 10 minutes until browned. Serve hot, cut in half and spread with butter.

Each scone is 10g CHO. 90 kcals.

PEANUT SCONES

Despite their name peanuts are not nuts at all, but legumes or pulses. They grow on a bush and the nuts mature below ground. They originate from South America and have been found in Peruvian tombs dating around 950 BC. Peanuts contain 24g of protein per 100g which makes them very nutritious: 100g of peanuts has the same amount of protein as a grilled lamb chop.

150g (5 oz) wholewheat flour
15g (½ oz) wheatgerm
100g (4 oz) ground peanuts
½ tsp bicarbonate of soda
1 tsp cream of tartar
½ tsp mixed spice
25g (1 oz) margarine
100g (4 oz) ripe banana,
  peeled
75–100ml (3–4 fl oz) low-fat
  natural yogurt

Makes 12 scones

Combine the wholewheat flour, wheatgerm, ground peanuts, bicarbonate of soda, cream of tartar and mixed spice in a large bowl. Rub the margarine into the flour mixture. Mash the banana with a fork and stir in. Add enough yogurt to form a soft malleable dough.

Remove the dough from the bowl and roll or pat out on a lightly floured wooden board or clean work top to a thickness of 1.2cm (½ in). Use a 6cm (2½ in) cutter to make 12 scones. Place on an ungreased baking tray and bake in a preheated oven gas mark 7/220°C/425°F for 15–20 minutes until they are well browned on top and underneath. Serve hot, cut in half and spread with butter.

Each scone is 10g CHO. 115 kcals.

LEMON SCONES

'The doctor is sure that my health is poor,
He says that I waste away;
So bring me a can of the shredded bran,
And a baleful of the toasted hay.'
(Walt Mason, late 19th century American humorist
                    and poet, in *Health Food*)

At last, a scone recipe with bran!

175g (6 oz) wholewheat flour
1g (25 oz) bran
½ tsp bicarbonate of soda
1 tsp cream of tartar
pinch of cinnamon, ground
  cloves and nutmeg
  (optional)
25g (1 oz) margarine
100g (4 oz) ripe pear, grated
1–2 tsp lemon zest
150ml (5 fl oz) skimmed milk

Makes 12 scones

Combine the flour, bran, bicarbonate of soda, cream of tartar and spices in a medium-sized bowl. Rub the margarine into the flour mixture. Stir in the grated pear and lemon zest, making sure they are spread evenly through the flour mixture. Use enough of the milk to bind the ingredients together to a soft dough.

Remove the dough from the bowl and roll out to a thickness of 0.5–1cm (¼–⅜ in). Cut into 6cm (2½ in) circles. The mixture makes 12 good-sized scones. Place them on an ungreased baking tray and bake in a preheated oven gas mark 8/230°C/450°F for about 10 minutes until evenly browned. Serve plain or with butter.

Each scone is 10g CHO. 70 kcals.

BARLEY LOAF

This loaf is quick to make as it is raised with bicarbonate of soda instead of yeast. The texture is more crumbly than an ordinary loaf of bread. If it is baked the evening before it will keep for the whole of the next day.

In ancient Rome barley was the special food of the gladiators and they were known in Latin as 'the barley-eaters'. By the Middle Ages in Europe barley bread was the staple of the peasants while the upper classes ate wheat. Bread made of barley flour and wheat flour could still be found in the mid-19th century in certain parts of the British Isles such as Wales and Cornwall, but today it has become a rarity.

Make sure that the barley you use is milled from the whole grain. It can be obtained from health food shops. This loaf can be made as a plain bread or with raisins.

Buttermilk, as its name suggests, is what is leftover in the churns from making butter. It works very well with a soda bread like this recipe because the lactic acid acts on the bicarbonate of soda and helps to lighten the dough.

300g (11 oz) barley flour
100g (4 oz) wholewheat flour
25g (1 oz) bran
2 tsp baking powder
1 tsp bicarbonate of soda
¼ tsp salt
50g (2 oz) margarine .
100g (4 oz) raisins, washed
    and dried (optional)
375–400ml (13–14 fl oz)
    buttermilk and skimmed
    milk mixed together

Makes 20 slices

Combine the flours and bran together in a large bowl. Mix the baking powder, bicarbonate of soda and salt and stir into the flours. Rub the margarine into the mixture lightly. If you are sweetening the loaf with raisins stir them in at this point. Slowly add the buttermilk and skimmed milk to the mixture to make a soft dough. Only add as much as is necessary to achieve this.

Divide the dough into two halves and place on a lightly floured wooden board or clean work top. Gently work them into two round loaves about 2.5cm (1 in) thick all the way round. Slash the tops with a knife and place them on a greased baking tin. Bake in a preheated oven gas mark 5/190°C/375°F for 35–40 minutes until they are browned all over. If you are leaving them overnight, wrap them up in a clean tea towel to keep the moisture in.

Each slice without raisins is 15g CHO. 100 kcals.
Each slice with raisins is 20g CHO. 110 kcals.

DROP SCONES

Using a griddle is a quicker way to cook a scone than in the oven because the heat is more direct. Griddles, or bake stones as they were traditionally known in some parts of England, are not always easy to come by and a suitable substitute is a heavy frying pan. I use a simple low-cost cast-iron one which is sold in a couple of the national household chain stores. To season one of these pans heat it gently and rub well with oil. Leave it to stand for a while and then wipe off the oil.
When cooking drop scones, heat the pan and oil it very lightly.

Do not overheat or the outside of the scone will burn before the heat has penetrated to the inside. Scones cooked on a griddle are rolled out more thinly than those baked in the oven. After using, wipe the inside of the pan with some kitchen paper and a little salt, rather than washing it up. Soaking a frying pan in water makes food more likely to stick next time it is used and to counteract this you would have to use extra oil.

The batter for the drop scones can be whizzed up in a few minutes.

90g (3½ oz) wholewheat flour
15g (½ oz) wheatgerm
½ tsp bicarbonate of soda
½ tsp cream of tartar
1 egg, lightly beaten
100ml (4 fl oz) buttermilk
100ml (4 fl oz) skimmed milk
a little oil for cooking

Makes 15 drop scones

Combine the flour and wheatgerm in a medium-sized bowl. Mix together the bicarbonate of soda and cream of tartar and add to the flour. Pour the egg into a well in the middle of the flour. Continue to beat until the egg gradually absorbs some of the flour. Add enough of the buttermilk and skimmed milk to make a smooth thick batter.

Heat the griddle or heavy frying pan and grease it very slightly with a little oil. Use a tablespoon to drop even quantities of the mixture on to the griddle. It should make 15 scones. When bubbles appear on the surface of the scones turn them over until browned on the other side. Serve hot with butter or jam.

2 drop scones are 10g CHO. 65 kcals.

SINGIN' HINNY

This recipe is based on the traditional griddle cake made in the north of England.

200g (7 oz) wholewheat flour
25g (1 oz) soya flour
2 tsp baking powder
25g (1 oz) butter
40g (1½ oz) currants
175–200ml (6–7 fl oz)
   low-fat natural yogurt

Combine the flour and baking powder together in a large bowl. Rub the butter into the mixture. Stir in the washed and dried currants and use as much yogurt as necessary to bind it into a soft dough.

Remove the dough from the bowl and roll out on a lightly floured board or work top to the same size as your griddle or large frying pan; prick the surface all over with a fork.

Heat and slightly grease the griddle. Cook the rolled-out dough on both sides until evenly browned. Traditionally this is cooked in one large piece, but you will probably find it easier to handle if you cut it into quarters. Eat hot spread with butter.

Each quarter is 45g CHO. 275 kcals.

OATCAKES

These taste good hot or cold. This recipe uses a mixture of oats and oat bran and germ as this increases the fibre content of the oatcakes. Bran from oats is one of the best sources of fibre. Soluble fibre dissolves in water and swells in the stomach to give a feeling of fullness which can reduce hunger. According to studies made by Dr James Anderson of Kentucky University, soluble fibre from oats also slows down the rate at which food is absorbed, which is beneficial for people with diabetes because it results in a stable blood sugar level. It was also found to reduce cholesterol levels.

If buying oatcakes, do read the list of ingredients carefully, because most brands I have come across include a sweetening agent. The traditional flavouring is just a pinch of salt, and you can spread something savoury or sweet on top.

50g (2 oz) oatmeal
50g (2 oz) oat germ and bran
   (if not available use
   oatmeal)
pinch of sea salt
1 tbs oil
about 50ml (2 fl oz) boiling
   water

Makes 16 triangular oatcakes

Combine the oatmeal, oat germ and bran and salt in a medium-sized bowl. Stir in the oil. Work in as much hot water as necessary to make a soft pastry.

Remove from the bowl and roll out thinly on a wooden board or work top. If the pastry is too moist, dust the board with oatmeal. Cut into 11cm (4½ in) circles and cut each one into four triangles. Cook on a greased griddle, making sure it is not smoking hot, for about 4 minutes on each side. The oatcakes should be firm, but not brown when cooked. Alternatively they can be baked on an ungreased tray in a preheated oven gas mark 3/170°C/325°F for 20–25 minutes.

3 oatcakes are 10g CHO. 95 kcals.

3 SPREADS AND TOPPINGS

The alternative food industry has had its greatest successes with sugar-free substitutes for sticky jams and nut spreads. Varieties that range from strawberry to Italian peach and lemon shred can now be found in many supermarkets.

The jams are made from fruit, pectin and fruit juice rather than sugar and fruit. Because of the easy access to manufactured jam it is not essential for sugar-free cooks to invest a lot of time making spreads. However, it is worth knowing the basic methods.

Nut spreads are often sweetened. In the USA up to 10 per cent of sugar can legally be added to manufactured peanut butter. Some sugar-free versions are available, although the end product differs greatly – to such an extent that one firm's crunchy peanut butter can be the answer to your dreams while their smooth version can seal your jaws in a cement-like vice.

The spreads in this section can be used on bread or double up as fillings in cakes. The fruit fillings can be stored in the fridge for up to a week. If they are made with a soft white cheese such as quark they should be consumed the same day.

Basic icing recipes are also given. Some cake and biscuit recipes refer specifically to a filling or topping while Children's Parties (see pages 181–7) gives ideas on how to use them to decorate birthday cakes.

PEANUT BUTTER

Peanuts, asserts the American food authority Dr Caroline Shreeve, are mildly aphrodisiac. They contain three amino acids which she claims improve sexual performance. She does not specify the amount of peanuts needed to achieve the desired effect – whether it is ounces, pounds or tonnes.

200g (7 oz) peanuts
2 tsp oil

Spread the peanuts out on a shallow baking dish and put in a preheated oven gas mark 4/180°C/350°F for 20–30 minutes until they are browned but not burnt. Grind the cooled roasted peanuts and oil in an electric coffee grinder until a paste is formed. Store in a glass jar in the fridge.

Peanut Butter is 17.5g CHO. 1230 kcals.

APRICOT–ALMOND SPREAD

This spread requires no cooking. The main benefits are protein from the almonds, vitamin A from the dried apricots and vitamin C from the apple.

75g (3 oz) dried apricots
75g (3 oz) whole almonds
spring water
1 medium apple weighing about 150g (5 oz), chopped

Place the dried apricots and almonds in a small bowl. Pour on as much spring water as is necessary to cover them and leave overnight. In the morning blend or process the apricots, nuts and water together with the chopped apple. (There is no need to peel the apple before chopping; simply wash and pat dry.) Blend until all the fruit and nuts have been broken down to a creamy paste. Pour into a glass jar and store in the fridge.

Apricot-Almond Spread is 50g CHO. 610 kcals.

PINEAPPLE CONSERVE

Pineapple conserve is first boiled and then combined with apple pectin to create a more jam-like consistency. Pectin can be made from other fruits such as lime. It can also be purchased from the chemist's.

Apple pectin
450g (1 lb) apples, including
  cores and peel
600ml (20 fl oz) water

Apple cores and peel, which are high in pectin, should be saved for this recipe.

Combine the ingredients in a heavy saucepan and boil for 30 minutes. Pour the liquid through a colander to separate it from the fruit. Boil it down to about 125ml (4½ fl oz). It can be stored in the fridge in a sealed jar.

Conserve
400g (14 oz) pineapple
  without skin, chopped
150g (5 oz) eating apple,
  grated
100ml (4 fl oz) apple juice,
  unsweetened
125ml (4½ fl oz) apple pectin

This conserve is blended before cooking, for speed. Liquidize the chopped pineapple, grated apple and apple juice, pour into a heavy stainless steel saucepan and boil for 10–12 minutes. Add the pectin and boil for a further 3–5 minutes. Most of the juice will be absorbed during the cooking. Remove from the heat. Pour into a prepared glass jar and store in the fridge.

Pineapple Conserve is 75g CHO. 300 kcals.

TAHINI–BANANA SPREAD

Tahini is made from sesame seeds and is a source of calcium.

Use a good quality tahini for this recipe – Greek brands are usually very suitable. The tahini in the jar should have quite a liquid texture.

50g (2 oz) banana, peeled
50g (2 oz) tahini
4 tbs orange juice, freshly
   squeezed

Mash the banana with a fork and combine with the tahini and orange juice to make a smooth paste. It can be used as a spread for bread or as a cream to put between two halves of a cake. It is best eaten the same day so only mix up as much as you need.

Tahini–Banana Spread is 20g CHO. 370 kcals.

CHERRY CREAM

This sweet-tasting cream can be used to sandwich two cakes together or spread on top of a cake.

75g (3 oz) cherries
1 tbs apple juice
75g (3 oz) skimmed milk
   quark

Destone the cherries. Blend with the apple juice to make a thick purée. Fold in the quark to make a deep pinkish-red cream.

Cherry Cream is 15g CHO. 100 kcals.

HAZELNUT–CAROB CREAM FILLING

75g (3 oz) hazelnuts, ground
25g (1 oz) carob powder
2 tbs orange juice, freshly
   squeezed
115g (4½ oz) skimmed milk
   quark
75g (3 oz) banana, peeled

Combine the ground hazelnuts and carob powder in a medium bowl. Stir in the orange juice, quark and mashed banana to make a thick cream that is ready to spread. Use the same day.

Total value is 40g CHO. 500 kcals.

CHESTNUT–SATSUMA CREAM FILLING

This rich creamy filling is ideal for filling a Swiss roll or a baked tart case. This gives enough to fill a 20cm (8 in) diameter pastry case. Use half the quantity for a Swiss roll.

4 satsumas
1 quantity Crème aux
   Marrons (see page 170)

Peel the satsumas and remove the white pith. Chop into small pieces with a sharp knife and add, together with any juice, to the Crème aux marrons. Stir together and it is ready to use.

Total value is 125g CHO. 660 kcals.

CAROB ICING

This creamy sweet icing quickly becomes firm. It is ideal for decorating cakes and biscuits and also freezes well.

25g (1 oz) butter or
   margarine
25g (1 oz) carob powder
75ml (3 fl oz) skimmed milk
15g (½ oz) ground almonds
1 tsp brandy or brandy
   essence (optional)

Prepare the icing by putting the margarine, carob powder and milk in a small saucepan. Slowly heat, stirring the ingredients all the time until a smooth liquid is formed. It should hardly boil. Take off the heat and add the ground almonds and brandy.

An alternative to ground almonds in this recipe is to use 15g (½ oz) finely ground porridge oats.

Carob Icing is 15g CHO. 365 kcals.

COCONUT ICING

This thin white icing absorbs any colour. The carbohydrate content is negligible, but it is high in saturated fat so use in small quantities.

50g (2 oz) coconut cream
150ml (5 fl oz) water
colouring (optional)

Heat the cut-up coconut cream and water in a medium-sized saucepan until the lumps of coconut cream have dissolved, forming a thickish white paste. Use plain or add colouring.

Coconut Icing is neg CHO. 165 kcals.

4 BISCUITS, BARS AND SWEET NOTHINGS

Biscuits come in all shapes and textures. Crescents, squares, circles and small balls can all be found piled up in the biscuit tin. Some are crunchy, others soft or hard. Everyone has their own idea of what their favourite biscuit should be. The ones given in this section are made from a dough and rolled into shapes, dropped by the spoonful onto trays, poured into flat tins and sliced into bars, or crisp pastries sandwiched together with creams.

Biscuits have different functions at different times. In the morning they are required to be substantial snacks and provide an extra supply of energy, while in the afternoon they are only required to keep you going till the evening meal.

MEDITERRANEAN HALF–MOONS

These half-moon-shaped biscuits with a firm cake-like texture are perfumed with the pungent aniseed.

25ml (1 fl oz) boiling water
25g (1 oz) prunes, stoned
100g (4 oz) wholewheat flour
50g (2 oz) carob powder
¾–1 tbs aniseed
25g (1 fl oz) oil
1 egg, lightly beaten
50g (2 oz) cottage cheese

Makes 20 biscuits

Pour the boiling water over the prunes and leave to stand for 15 minutes. Combine the flour, carob powder and aniseed in a medium bowl. Add the oil, egg and cottage cheese that has been sieved or put through a food mill to remove the lumps.

Put the prunes and small amount of liquid in an electric coffee grinder and blend. Fold into the flour mixture and work to form a moist dough.

To make the dough into equal-sized crescents divide it into half and roll each piece into a long sausage about 50cm (20 in) long. Cut each one into ten 5cm (20 in) lengths. This will give a total of 20. Gently bend each piece into a half-moon or crescent, making the ends slightly pointed, so that the crescent is a little thicker in the middle. Place them on a greased baking tray and bake in a preheated oven gas mark 3/170°C/325°F for 15–20 minutes until firm.

1 biscuit is 5g CHO. 45 kcals.

SESAME SQUARES

The sesame seeds used in the recipes in this book are very small, brown and are unhulled, which means they still have their mineral-rich outer covering. Sesame seeds are rich in linoleic unsaturated fatty acids. These are known as essential fatty acids because the body cannot make them itself and is dependent for its supply on foods containing them.

50g (2 oz) dried dates, chopped
100ml (4 fl oz) water
100g (4 oz) sesame seeds
50g (2 oz) wholewheat flour
50g (2 oz) ground almonds
zest of 1 small lemon
juice of half a lemon (about 1½ tbs)
1 egg, lightly beaten

Makes 18 squares

Put the dates and water in a small saucepan on a low heat and cook till the water is absorbed and the dates have become mushy. Leave to cool. Combine the sesame seeds, flour and ground almonds in a medium bowl. Stir in the lemon zest, juice and date paste. Fold the egg into the sesame flour and date mixture. This will give a thick paste-like texture.

Oil a 22.5cm (9 in) square baking dish and spread the mixture evenly over the base of the dish using the back of a spoon to flatten the surface.

Bake in a preheated oven gas mark 4/

180°C/350°F for 15–20 minutes until evenly browned. Cut into 18 squares when cool.

Each Sesame Square is 5g CHO. 70 kcals.

CHESTNUT FUDGE FINGERS

Chestnuts are a welcome winter treat. This is the time of year when you see chestnut sellers in the streets of Central London warming themselves by their hot furnaces in between urging bags of roasted nuts into your gloved hands.

Unlike many other nuts, chestnuts are high in carbohydrates, but low in oils. They contain 500mg of potassium per 100g and include small amounts of calcium and magnesium and some of the B vitamins.

Chestnut purée can be bought in tins or you can make it yourself. If using fresh chestnuts peel them then boil until soft and all the cooking water is absorbed. Then sieve or put through a food mill. Out of season it is possible to obtain dried chestnuts, but these have to be boiled for a considerable length of time.

100g (4 oz) dried dates, chopped
100ml (4 fl oz) water
100g (4 oz) wholewheat flour
50g (2 oz) soya flour
25g (1 oz) wheatgerm
1 tsp bicarbonate of soda
2 tsp cream of tartar
200ml (7 fl oz) low-fat natural yogurt
1 tbs rum or 1 tsp rum essence
25g (1 oz) soya flakes soaked in 1 dessertspoon orange juice
100g (4 oz) chestnut purée, unsweetened

Makes 16 servings

Put the dates and water in a small saucepan and cook over a low heat until the water is absorbed and the dates have become mushy. Combine the wholewheat flour, soya flour, wheatgerm, bicarbonate of soda and cream of tartar in a medium bowl. Fold in the date mixture and yogurt. Add the rum, soya flakes and chestnut purée. This makes a creamy texture.

Pour into a greased and floured 20cm (8 in) square baking tin and bake in a preheated oven gas mark 4/ 190°C/350°F for 30–40 minutes until evenly browned. Cut into 16 fingers.

Each biscuit is 15g CHO. 75 kcals.

OAT SNACKS

This is a filling biscuit for a mid-morning snack. It should provide enough even energy to keep you going until lunch as the oats are high in soluble fibre which aids slow absorption of food in the body. The tofu provides protein and the carob gives sweetness and more fibre.

100g (4 oz) porridge oats
100g (4 oz) oat bran and germ
50g (2 oz) carob powder
50g (2 oz) dried dates
100ml (4 fl oz) water
100g (4 oz) banana, peeled
200g (7 oz) firm tofu
50ml (2 fl oz) skimmed milk or soya milk

Makes 15 biscuits

Combine the oats, oat bran and germ and carob powder in a medium bowl. Put the banana and tofu through a hand mill or blend in a liquidizer and combine with the dry ingredients. Add as much of the milk as necessary to make a pastry dough.

Pat or roll out on a floured board or work top to a thickness of about 1cm (½ in). Use a 5cm (2 in) cutter to make 15 thick rounds. Place on an ungreased baking tray and bake in a preheated oven gas mark 3/ 170°C/325°F for 30–40 minutes until lightly browned and firm.

Each biscuit is 15g CHO. 75 kcals.

SESAME OAT BARS

Either allergies are becoming more common or people's awareness of them has radically increased – I am forever being asked for recipes that exclude one sensitive foodstuff or another. These bars are suitable for a number of exclusion diets because they contain no egg, flour or milk.

Sesame seeds are rich in calcium, with 815mg per 100g. It is difficult to eat many in cakes, but savoury foods such as tahini, which is made of ground sesame seeds, or gomasio, a Japanese condiment of toasted ground sesame seeds mixed with a little salt, are a more concentrated source.

50g (2 oz) prunes, stoned and chopped
25g (1 oz) dried dates, chopped
100ml (4 fl oz) water
100g (4 oz) porridge oats
100g (4 oz) sesame seeds
100g (4 oz) soya bean flakes
25g (1 oz) sultanas, chopped
100ml (4 fl oz) orange juice, unsweetened
100ml (4 fl oz) soya milk

Makes 20 bars

Heat the prunes and dates in a small saucepan with the water over a low heat until all the water is absorbed and a mushy paste is formed.

Combine the oats, sesame seeds and soya bean flakes. Add the sultanas, date and prune paste, orange juice and soya milk to make a moist mixture. Spread the mixture evenly over the base of a 22.5cm (9 in) square greased baking tin. Bake in a preheated oven gas mark 4/ 180°C/350°F for 25–30 minutes until browned all over. Cut into 20 slices.

Each bar is 10g CHO. 85 kcals.

CAROB FUDGE SQUARES

Carob is widely used in health food circles as an alternative to chocolate, but it does have its own unique taste. The reasons that a sugar-free cook prefers carob to chocolate are that it contains fibre, is high in natural sugar and remarkably low in fat, with only 1/34 of the fat content in chocolate. In addition carob is free of the two stimulants caffeine and theobromine which are found in chocolate. (Theobromine has been linked with migraine and allergic responses; caffeine stimulates the central nervous system and taken in excess can become addictive.) Carob is also bursting with such minerals as calcium, magnesium, potassium and phosphorus.

These creamy squares are messy to eat, but worth getting sticky fingers for.

100g (4 oz) wholewheat flour
100g (4 oz) porridge oats
½ tsp mixed spice (optional)
50ml (2 fl oz) oil
½ tsp almond essence
1 medium ripe pear, grated

Combine the flour, oats and mixed spice. Stir in the oil and almond essence. Add the pear and work into a moist dough. Divide the dough in half. Pat one piece with the flat of your fingers over the base of a 20cm

Filling
4 eating apples weighing
  about 500g (1lb 4 oz)
25g (1 oz) dried dates,
  chopped
100ml (4 fl oz) water
15g (½ oz) carob powder
2 egg yolks

Makes 20 small squares

(8 in) square greased baking tin. Pat the second piece out on a similar-sized tin, but as it will eventually be broken into large crumbs you do not have to work it so carefully.

Bake in a preheated oven gas mark 5/ 190°C/375°F for 25 minutes until the pieces of pastry are evenly browned.

While the pastry base is cooking slice the apples into a saucepan together with the dates and water. Bring to the boil and simmer until the fruit is softened. Stir in the carob powder about a minute before you remove the apples from the heat. Pour all these ingredients into a blender to make a thick purée. Return the carob, apple and date purée to the pan and add the broken-up pieces of the second sheet of baked pastry. Heat the fruit purée and crumbs for about a minute so that it is hot, but not boiling.

Lightly beat the two egg yolks with a fork. Pour the fruit mixture over the egg yolks, stirring as you add it to the eggs. (If the fruit mixture is too hot you will have fried eggs and that should be avoided.) The filling takes on a lovely creamy texture. Pour it evenly over the first pastry base and when cold chill in the fridge.

Each square is 10g CHO. 80 kcals.

CAROB HAZELNUT SLICE

Hazelnuts grow mostly in Turkey and Europe. They contain some of the important minerals – including potassium and zinc – with a sizeable 21mg of vitamin E in every 100g. Culpeper, the 17th century herbalist, recommended using the pounded nuts or nut milk for treating a persistent cough. When mixed with a little pepper, this was thought to 'draw rheum from the head'.

1 quantity Sweet Seed Pastry
   (see page 91–2)

Filling
150g (5 oz) finely chopped
   hazelnuts
50g (2 oz) carob powder
75g (3 oz) dried apricots,
   finely chopped
150ml (5 fl oz) water
2 egg whites

Makes 20 fingers

Use your fingers to press the pastry over the base of a 20×25cm (8×10 in) baking dish. Bake in a preheated oven gas mark 4/180°C/350°F for 10 minutes until lightly browned around the edges.

Combine the hazelnuts and carob powder. Put the dried apricots and water in a small saucepan and heat until the water is absorbed and the apricots have become paste-like. Cool. Mix the apricot paste with the nuts and carob. Whisk the egg whites to stiff snowy peaks and fold in to make a moist paste.

Spread this mixture evenly over the half-baked pastry, return to the oven and bake for a further 10 minutes. It only needs to be baked enough so that it sets. If it cooks for too long the hazelnut will become hard and not chewy.

Cut into fingers for serving when cold.

2 fingers are 10g CHO. 150 kcals.

CAROB ALMOND BALLS

These small soft carob balls coated in white coconut are a pleasant introduction to carob. Carob powder is made from a crescent-shaped pod that is found growing in the Near East and southern Mediterranean lands. It has been used for thousands of years. References to it have been found in ancient Sumerian texts and the Romans called it 'carobi'. It is also known as St John's Bread after the time John the Baptist wandered in the wilderness and used this mineral-rich pod as a means of survival. The carob that we buy in the shops has been roasted and ground a couple of times.

75g (3 oz) dried dates, chopped
25g (1 oz) dried prunes, stoned and chopped
150ml (5 fl oz) water
250g (9 oz) ground almonds
50g (2 oz) carob powder
3 egg whites, stiffly beaten
25g (1 oz) desiccated coconut, unsweetened, for decoration

Makes 27 Carob Almond Balls

Heat the dates, prunes and water in a small saucepan over a low heat until the water is absorbed. Be careful that the mixture does not burn. The dried fruit should become very mushy. If the texture does not become paste-like blend the dried fruit. Mix the ground almonds and carob powder together. Add the date and prune mixture. Fold in the egg whites to make a moist but stiff consistency.

Divide the mixture into three equal portions and use a teaspoon to measure out 9 equal pieces from each portion. Roll these between the palms of your hands into small balls. Place on a greased tray and bake in a preheated oven gas mark 3/ 170°C/325°F for 20–25 minutes until lightly browned. While still warm remove from the tray and roll them in a plate of coconut. Only a little of the coconut will stick to the balls so sprinkle some over the top as well.

3 balls are 10g CHO. 215 kcals.

CAROB SECRETS

These crunchy carob treats taste very like chocolate and are always a pleasant surprise to guests bravely trying carob for the first time. Carob contains 46 per cent natural sugar which makes this a very sweet treat.

75g (3 oz) flaked almonds
75g (3 oz) sultanas
scant 25g (scant 1 oz) carob powder
50ml (2 fl oz) water
½ tsp vanilla essence
18 small paper cases

Makes 18 Carob Secrets

Chop the flaked almonds into halves. Wash, drain and chop the sultanas into thirds or very briefly chop in an electric grinder – the danger with an electric machine is that it can quickly reduce the sultanas to a pulp.

Put the carob powder, water and vanilla essence in a small saucepan and heat on a low light until the carob powder has dissolved. Add the sultanas and flaked almonds to the carob mixture. Stir with a small wooden spoon, crushing the flakes a little more.

When the sultanas and almond flakes are mixed together and well coated with the carob sauce put a heaped teaspoon in each of the 18 miniature paper cases. Leave to chill in the fridge for one hour before serving.

They are delicious after a meal or as a special sweet treat.

3 carob secrets are 10g CHO. 110 kcals.

CINNAMON DROPS

'And lucent syrops, tinct with cinnamon', wrote Keats in The Eve of St Agnes, *evoking the exotic imagery conjured up by this fragrant Eastern spice to hint at the beauty of his sleeping love. The origins of cinnamon are decidedly unromantic. It is the dried inner bark of a small tree from the East Indies and was among the first*

commodities traded from the East to the Mediterranean, mentioned repeatedly in the Bible and an indispensable adjunct to worship in Solomon's temple.

125g (4½ oz) dried dates, chopped
100ml (4 fl oz) water
225g (8 oz) ground almonds
4 tsp cinnamon
2 egg whites, stiffly beaten

Makes 27 drops

Heat the dates and water in a small saucepan until all the water is absorbed and a paste is formed. Blend in an electric coffee grinder to a smooth consistency. Leave to cool.

Combine the ground almonds and cinnamon in a mixing bowl then fold in the date mixture. Bind with the egg whites. To shape the drops moisten the palms of your hands with cold water and roll the mixture into 27 small balls. Place them on a lightly greased baking tray.

Bake in a preheated oven gas mark 3/ 170°C/325°F for 20–25 minutes, so that they are slightly brown on the outside and underneath. The drops should be firm outside, but with a chewy texture inside.

3 drops are 10g CHO. 180 kcals.

PINE AND ALMOND CRESCENTS

Pine nuts, said Culpeper, are 'excellent restoratives in consumption and after long illness'. They are also a light and delicious nut which makes a welcome addition to sweet and savoury dishes. It is worth comparing prices in a few shops before purchasing because there is usually quite a disparity.

The almond dough is quick to make, but rolling the crescents in a plate of pine nuts and ensuring that the nuts become embedded on the outside of the crescents can take at least 15 minutes so it is worth sitting down comfortably with an interesting radio programme to listen to.

This recipe uses very few dates, but still tastes quite sweet. The reason for this is that the nuts themselves are naturally sweet.

50g (2 oz) dried dates
50ml (2 fl oz) water
150g (5 oz) ground almonds
juice and zest of half a lemon
1 egg white, stiffly beaten
100g (4 oz) pine nuts

Makes 15 biscuits

Put the dates and water in a small saucepan and simmer on a low heat until the water is absorbed. Allow to cool then purée to a smooth paste.

Combine the date purée with the ground almonds and lemon juice and zest in a mixing bowl. Add the egg white to the almond mixture to make a sticky paste.

Spread out the pine nuts on a large plate. Take a generous teaspoonful of the mixture and roll it into a sausage in the palm of your hand. Roll it in a plate of pine nuts so that it becomes encrusted with them. As you lay the sausage shape on a greased baking tray curve it into a crescent shape making the ends slightly narrower than the middle. Coating with the pine nuts makes the crescents larger than the original piece of almond dough.

Bake in a preheated oven gas mark 3/170°C/325°F for 10–15 minutes until very lightly browned.

3 crescents are 10g CHO. 315 kcals.

PRUNE AND PEAR DROPS

These are very moist titbits.

50g (2 oz) dried prunes,
    stoned and finely chopped
50ml (2 fl oz) water
75g (3 oz) ground almonds
¼ tsp mixed spice
1 egg white, stiffly beaten
200g (7 oz) pear

Makes 16 Prune and Pear Drops

Put the prunes and water in a small saucepan and simmer on a low heat until the water is absorbed. Combine the softened prunes with the ground almonds and mixed spice in a mixing bowl. Grate the pear into the almond mixture and stir; fold in the egg white to make a thick paste.

Place 16 dessertspoons of the mixture on a greased baking tray. Bake in a preheated oven gas mark 3/170°C/325°F for 20 minutes until browned.

4 drops are 10g CHO. 150 kcals.

CINNAMON HAZELNUT STICKS

These are an all-time favourite. They look like they have come out of a patisserie, but are quite simple to make.

50g (2 oz) dried dates, finely chopped
75ml (3 fl oz) water
75g (3 oz) ground hazelnuts
75g (3 oz) ground almonds
½ tsp cinnamon
2 egg whites, stiffly beaten
1 quantity Carob Icing (see page 56)

Makes 20 small sticks

Put the dates and water in a small saucepan and simmer on a low heat until the water has been absorbed. Mash with a fork to make a paste. Combine the hazelnuts, almonds and cinnamon in a mixing bowl. Add the date paste to the nuts, working it in with a spoon. Use the egg whites to bind the nut dough.

Either roll the mixture in your hands to make the sticks or for a more professional finish pipe them on a lightly greased baking tray. I use an icing bag without any of the nozzles at the end, but only the plastic holder which is about 1.3cm (⅝ in) diameter. Pipe out the sticks to about 7.5cm (3 in) in length. The mixture makes 20 sticks. Bake in a preheated oven gas mark 3/170°C/325°F for 15–20 minutes until lightly browned.

When cool, dip each end of the sticks in Carob Icing as it begins to thicken. They look very tempting.

4 cinnamon hazelnut sticks are 10g CHO. 245 kcals.

SUNFLOWER CHEWS

50g (2 oz) dried dates,
   chopped
25g (1 oz) prunes, stoned and
   chopped
100ml (4 fl oz) water
75g (3 oz) sunflower seeds
15g (½ oz) unsweetened
   desiccated coconut
25g (1 oz) peanut butter

Makes 12 Sunflower Chews

Put the dates and prunes in a small
saucepan with the water and cook
over a low heat until the water has
been absorbed. Mash with a fork to
make a thick paste.

Grind the sunflower seeds in an
electric coffee grinder. Put them in a
bowl and mix with the coconut, date
and prune paste and peanut butter.

Roll the mixture into 12 balls,
moistening the palms of your hands
with cold water. Chill in the fridge
for a couple of hours before serving.

2 chews are 10g CHO. 140 kcals.

PECAN FUDGE

50g (2 oz) dried dates
100ml (4 fl oz) water
75g (3 oz) pecan nuts,
   coarsely chopped
1 dessertspoon tahini

Makes 8 portions

Put the dates in a small saucepan
with the water and cook over a low
heat until the water has been
absorbed. Mash with a fork to make
a thick paste.

Remove the pan from the heat. Stir in
the nuts and tahini and mix well.
Press into an 18cm (7 in) diameter
baking tin. Leave in the fridge for
one hour to chill. Cut into 8 chunks
and serve.

Each portion is 5g CHO. 85 kcals.

CAROB APRICOT TREATS

Making your own carob-coated fruit is quick and simple. Be sure to use a good quality carob bar for a ravishing result.

All carob chocolates are high in fat and contain as many or more calories than milk chocolate, so keep them for special occasions.

Make sure that you use dried apricots that are soft and plump and not wizened and hard.

50g (2 oz) carob bar
100g (4 oz) whole dried
  apricots

Makes about 16–18 treats

Cut the carob bar into small pieces and place in a bowl in a pan filled with boiling water. Leave until it has melted. Be very careful that no water gets into the bowl. As soon as the carob has melted dip the individual apricots into the bowl and coat them all the way round. Leave to harden on a sheet of greaseproof paper or a marble slab. Store in the fridge until needed.

About 3 Treats are 10g CHO. 80 kcals.

MARZIPAN

This recipe uses ground almonds and a fig paste, but if this becomes too expensive it is possible to substitute fine oatmeal for 25g (1 oz) of the ground almonds. The quantities would then be 50g (2 oz) ground almonds and 25g (1 oz) fine oatmeal. Everything else remains the same.

The taste of this marzipan is close to that of the sugar variety. The texture is not fine enough for modelling detailed shapes, but does work well with larger forms (see Marzipan Mice and Marzipan Fruit, below).

50g (2 oz) dried figs
50ml (2 fl oz) water
½ tsp almond essence
  colouring (optional)
75g (3 oz) ground almonds

Heat the dried figs and water in a pan until all the water is absorbed. Blend to a smooth paste.

When the mixture has cooled add the

almond essence and any colouring if used. Work in the ground almonds until a paste is formed. Wrap with greaseproof paper and chill in the fridge for 30 minutes before using.

This recipe is 30g CHO. 530 kcals.

MARZIPAN FRUIT AND MARZIPAN MICE

Add the colouring to the ground almonds before mixing them into the fig paste. A natural colouring is available from health food shops. Generous amounts of colouring will have to be used because the colour of the fig paste is brown.

Marzipan Fruit

Strawberries – use red marzipan. Work the pieces of marzipan into the conical shape typical of strawberries and stick green pumpkin seeds into the sides for strawberry seeds.
Apples – use green marzipan. Work it into round shapes and use a clove as a pungent stalk.
Stuffed dates – roll the green marzipan into oval shapes. Cut fresh dates in half and remove the stones. Place a green oval in each date half. This dish is worthy of Scheherazade and the tales of a thousand and one nights!

Marzipan Mice
double quantity of marzipan

Prepare the marzipan paste. Use the natural colour or make it slightly pink. Divide it into 8 equal pieces for 8 mice. From each one take a small piece of the marzipan and roll it into a ball for the head. Squeeze two little ears from the top of the head. Insert a couple of small raisins for eyes. Roll the rest of the marzipan into a sausage shape and attach to the head. Flatten the underneath of this shape so that it will sit on a flat surface. Cut a piece of coloured string for the tail and push it into the end of the body.

Repeat this process with the other 7 pieces of marzipan.

These are very popular with children and are something they can help to make. Decorative cardboard boxes such as those from herb tea make a suitable 'home' for the mice.

Each mouse is 7.5g CHO. 135 kcals.

5 SALADS

Sugar is not the first ingredient that comes to mind when you think of salads. But a surprisingly large number of dressings contain sweetener of some kind – and it is up to you to keep your salads as healthy as they look.

Salads are multi-purpose dishes. They can serve as a complete meal eaten with bread, as a side dish with a main course, or as an appetizer. One of their attractions is that they take little time to make – vegetables are washed, chopped, sliced or grated, and are eaten either as they are or with a dressing.

Commercial brands of mayonnaise and salad dressing include sugar, but there is no need to include it when you make your own. It does not improve the taste nor do dressings require sugar to emulsify. Emulsions are the combining of one liquid with another which cannot evenly mix, such as oil with water.

The other type of sweetness associated with salads is when fresh fruit or dried fruit are combined with vegetables to give a sweet and savoury taste. This is a combination that I enjoy occasionally, but not every day.

Salads provide great opportunities for experimentation. By judiciously adding grated or chopped apple, a handful of raisins, chopped dried apricots, chunks of pineapple or mango you can achieve very unusual effects. If you have to watch your calorie or carbohydrate intake, remember to use fruit sparingly.

Salad dressings

The NACNE (National Advisory Committee on Nutrition Education) report recommended fat consumption to be reduced to 34 per cent of total intake for everyone over the age of five. Dressings made with oil provide a useful source of fat for young children, particularly if the family follows a low-fat regime. My own under-five-year-old has a saucer of dressing every day made from olive oil with a splash of vinegar, in which she dips raw carrots, cucumber and green beans plus various parts of herself.

Oils used in dressings
Olive oil, which is high in mono-unsaturated fats, has been used for thousands of years in Mediterranean countries and is credited with relieving constipation and, in some cases, dissolving gallstones. The latest research suggests that it also helps in combating heart disease.

Sesame seed oil is high in polyunsaturated fats and contains 41g per 100ml linoleic acid, an essential fatty acid. The human body cannot manufacture it itself and it is important that it is included in the diet. Severe lack of linoleic acid leads to skin conditions, poor wound healing and anaemia.

Sesame seed oil is recommended by macrobiotics, while ayurvedics advocate rubbing it into your scalp. I prefer mine in salads.

Sunflower seed oil contains over half its oil in the form of polyunsaturates and a liberal dose of linoleic acid (58g per 100ml); the amount depends upon whether it is grown in a hot or cold climate.

Safflower oil contains three quarters of its oil in polyunsaturated form and contains 73g linoleic acid per 100ml.

Check the label to see if the oil has been cold pressed rather than produced at a high temperature; heat affects the composition of the oil. Cold-pressed oils have to be stored carefully in a cool, dark place or in the fridge. They are rich in nutrients and react with light and heat, oxydize with the air, and can become rancid if stored too long. Oils pressed under great heat remain more stable, but at the expense of their nutritional benefit.

No dressing will compensate for old, tired vegetables so always use the freshest available.

MAYONNAISE

The French invented mayonnaise and ought to know how to make it. Why then do English, American, German and other cookery writers insist on polluting this condiment with sugar? It may be that early cookery writers were subtly or unsubtly influenced by the sugar industry and the low price of sugar in the UK and the US; this dependence on sugar may also have something to do with the general tastelessness of the Anglo-American cuisine.

Eggs, the all-important ingredient in mayonnaise, contain such emulsifiers as lecithin and cholesterol which help to stabilize the mayonnaise emulsion. Use eggs that are at room temperature rather than straight from the fridge as this will make it easier for the mayonnaise to emulsify.

2 egg yolks
1 tsp mustard
freshly ground black pepper
sea salt (optional)
150ml (5 fl oz) olive oil
150ml (5 fl oz) sunflower oil
1 tbs white wine vinegar or 1
   tbs lemon juice

Put the egg yolks, mustard, pepper and salt in a bowl. Using either a whisk, hand held or electric, or even a fork, whisk the egg yolks lightly then add the oil drop by drop to begin with, whisking all the time. Gradually the mayonnaise will thicken. At this point you can start adding a little more oil each time, but keep on beating. The amount of oil you use may differ slightly each time you make this recipe so when the mayonnaise has the desired thickness add the vinegar or lemon juice to give a sharp taste. Finally add a few more drops of oil.

The mayonnaise can be stored in a glass jar in the fridge.

Mayonnaise is neg CHO. 2920 kcals.

VINAIGRETTE OR FRENCH DRESSING

freshly ground black pepper
sea salt (optional)
6 tbs oil
1½–2 tbs wine or cider
   vinegar

Season the oil then whisk in the vinegar until the texture thickens. If you are making a large quantity shake the dressing in a half-filled closed jar until it is ready. Store in the jar in the fridge.

Dressing is neg CHO. 825 kcals.

Variations:
– Add ½–1 tsp mustard.
– Add fresh or dried herbs to the dressing.

MEDITERRANEAN DRESSING

6 tbs oil
3 tbs lemon juice, freshly
    squeezed
freshly ground black pepper
sea salt (optional)

Combine all the ingredients and whisk well. Chopped parsley goes well mixed with this dressing.

Dressing is neg CHO. 810 kcals.

PEANUT-CARROT SALAD

75g (3 oz) raw peanuts
1 tbs sesame seeds, toasted
300g (11 oz) carrots, grated
25g (1 oz) sultanas
1 quantity Mediterranean
    Dressing (see above)

Makes 4 servings

Roast the peanuts on a shallow dish in a preheated ovengas mark 4/ 180°C/350°F. Leave to cool. Toast the sesame seeds for a minute or two under the grill so that they are lightly browned.

Combine the carrots, roasted peanuts, sultanas and toasted sesame seeds. Pour the Mediterranean Dressing over the salad and leave to stand for an hour before serving.

Each serving is 10g CHO. 255 kcals.

CHICORY SALAD

One sunny weekend in February I visited a friend and her daughter in Paris. She made this superb salad using green tarragon mustard in the dressing. The French call chicory endive and endive chicory. It took us some time to agree on what we were eating.

4 chicory heads
1 medium eating apple
75–100g (3–4 oz) walnuts
2 sticks of celery
Vinaigrette Dressing (see p.000)
½–1 tsp mustard (use tarragon mustard if available)

Makes 4 servings

Wash the chicory heads. Chop them into slices and place in a salad bowl. Wash and chop the apple. Chop the walnuts into halves or quarters and add to the bowl, together with the chopped celery.

Add the mustard to the Vinaigrette Dressing. Quickly toss the salad in this before the chicory and apples turn brown.

Each serving is 5g CHO. 345 kcals.

ORANGE AND CHINESE CABBAGE SALAD

The sesame seed oil gives a very distinctive nutty flavour to this salad.

1 small Chinese cabbage weighing about 500g (1 lb 2 oz)
1 small orange weighing about 150g (5 oz)
grated peel of half an orange

Dressing
6 tbs sesame seed oil
3 tbs orange juice
2 tbs lemon juice
freshly ground black pepper
sea salt (optional)

Makes 4 servings

Wash the Chinese cabbage and slice into shreds. Peel the orange carefully. Put half the rind to one side for grating. Remove all the pith from the outside of the orange and cut the flesh into thin slices. Add to the cabbage.

Combine the dressing ingredients and pour over the salad. Toss, and garnish with the grated orange rind.

Each serving is 10g CHO. 245 kcals.

6 CHUTNEYS AND SPICED FRUIT

Chutneys, relishes, spiced fruit and vegetables are a piquant and colourful accompaniment to plain dishes such as meat, fish or pies. Chutneys are an English version of the Indian *catni* brought over in the days of the Empire. The Indians do not invariably sweeten their chutney although sugar was available to them 1000 years before it came to Europe. Why then have British cookery writers from the 19th century to the present day found it impossible to make chutney without sugar? Even in the Middle East, famous for its syrupy cakes and early use of sugar, fruit and vegetables are pickled in vinegar and salt without added sweetener.

Because Western palates have become accustomed to sweetened condiments, most of the recipes in this section are sweetened despite the logical and ethnic indication to the contrary.

The fruit and vegetables in pickles and chutneys are not preserved by the sugar, but by the acid in the vinegar which discourages the growth of bacteria. Another method of preservation is to use a brine solution of salt and water strong enough to prevent the growth of unwanted bacteria, but weak enough to allow the growth of bacteria that produce lactic acid. This method is used in many Chinese and Japanese fermented pickles.

A few tips for making chutneys and pickles:

– Use a stainless steel saucepan because the vinegar can interact in a harmful way with metals such as iron or copper.
– Choose fresh unblemished fruit that is not overripe.
– Jars should be air-tight.
– Lids should not be made of uncovered metal.

Commercially produced sugar-free chutneys and ketchups are available in health food shops and specialist Indian grocers. Some of the firms which make these, however, are still small and do not have nationwide distribution.

PINEAPPLE DATE CHUTNEY

Pickling spice is a mixture of spices such as coriander, mustard seeds, peppercorns, allspice, bay leaves, ginger and chillies. It can be bought ready mixed.

When removing the skin from the pineapple make sure that no sharp spiky bits are left on the fruit.

600g (1lb 5 oz) fresh
   pineapple, without skin
175g (6 oz) onions, peeled
350g (12 oz) eating apples
40g (1½ oz) dried dates
75g (3 oz7 raisins
225ml (8 fl oz) cider vinegar
1 tsp pickling spice

Slice the pineapple into small chunky pieces and put on one side.

Put the finely chopped onions, apples, dates and raisins in a saucepan and cover with the vinegar. Tie the pickling spice in a muslin bag and add to the saucepan. Simmer on a low heat for half an hour. You might need to add a little water from time to time so that there is enough moisture for the fruit and onion to cook in.

Add the chopped pineapple and continue simmering for a further 45 minutes, always making sure there is enough liquid in the pan. Remove the pickling spice. Pour the chutney into a glass jar and seal. Store in the fridge.

Chutney is 180g CHO. 740 kcals.

FRENCH–CANADIAN CHUTNEY

The gracious mother of an old friend of mine who looks as if she has spent her entire life sipping tea out of bone china cups has actually spent most of her life in exotic locations from the Caribbean to the Seychelles. After the Second World War she lived for a couple of years on a chicken farm near the French-Canadian town of Cherbourg. The local radio station used to announce each morning the names of the inhabitants who had died the night before, then proceed to give traditional French-Canadian recipes. This is one that she saved for me.

700g (1lb 9 oz) tomatoes
125g (4½ oz) ripe plums, chopped
275g (10 oz) peaches, chopped
300g (11 oz) pears, chopped
225g (8 oz) onions, chopped very small
1 large green pepper
75ml (3 fl oz) cider vinegar
75ml (3 fl oz) apple juice, unsweetened
50g (2 oz) raisins
½ tsps sea salt
1 tsp pickling spice

Pour boiling water over the tomatoes and leave them to stand for 30 seconds. Pierce the skins with a sharp knife and peel. Chop into small pieces and put in a medium-sized stainless steel saucepan. Unless the skins of the plums, peaches and pears seem to be particularly thick they do not need removing as they become soft during cooking. Chop the onion into very small pieces. Cut the pepper open and remove all the seeds. Chop into small slices. Add all these ingredients to the pan.

Add the vinegar, apple juice, raisins and salt. Tie the pickling spice in a muslin bag and add to the pan.

Bring quickly to the boil and then simmer on a low heat for 1½–2 hours. Stir frequently as this chutney can catch easily. If there appears to be too much liquid at the end of the cooking time remove most of the fruit and vegetables and boil the liquid quickly so that it is reduced.

The chutney can be bottled directly in glass jars or it can be puréed if you prefer a smoother texture. Store in the fridge.

Chutney is 130g CHO. 565 kcals.

MANGO CHUTNEY

1 small clove garlic
pinch of cayenne
¼ tsp coriander seeds
¼ tsp ginger
¼ tsp cumin seeds
¼ tsp turmeric
150ml (5 fl oz) cider vinegar
150ml (5 fl oz) unsweetened
   apple juice
50g (2 oz) raisins
2 ripe mangoes weighing
   about 550–600g (1lb 4 oz
   –1lb 5 oz)

Squeeze the garlic through a garlic press. If the spices are in seed form pound them with a pestle and mortar or grind them in a small electric coffee grinder. Combine all the ingredients except the mangoes in a heavy stainless steel saucepan. Bring to the boil and then cook on a low heat for 15 minutes.

Peel the mangoes and cut them into small chunks. Add to the simmering spiced and sweetened vinegar and cook on a low heat for a further 15 minutes until the mango is cooked but still firm. Pour into glass jars. Store in the fridge.

Chutney is 110g CHO. 440 kcals.

SPICED MELON AND PEARS

Make this chutney when melons are in season towards the end of the summer. The ones that are sold in the winter do not have such a full sweet taste and will not contribute much in the way of flavour. Although melons are over 90 per cent water they still contain a number of minerals and vitamins such as potassium, magnesium and vitamin C, a trace of E and a few of the B vitamins.

450g (1 lb) ripe pears, finely chopped
50g (2 oz) dried dates, finely chopped
150ml (5 fl oz) white wine vinegar
1 tsp pickling spice
1 large honeydew or galia melon weighing about 1kg (2lb 7 oz)

Put the pears and dates in a stainless steel saucepan with the vinegar. Add pickling spice wrapped in a muslin bag. Simmer on a low light until the pears and dates are very soft. This takes about an hour and you may need to add a little extra water while they are simmering. When most of the liquid is absorbed remove the pickling spice and add the melon cut into chunks and cook for 15–20 minutes. Pour into a glass jar. Store in the fridge when cold.

Spiced melon is 100g CHO. 390 kcals.

7 PASTRIES, PIES AND TARTS

Pastry is an important starting-point for many kinds of dish. It can serve as a container for a sweet filling or a savoury one, for a main course or a dessert. When pastry is made with wholewheat grains it provides a source of high fibre which contains all the original nutrients. Pastry can be made from many different combinations: wheat flour and margarine, wheat flour and yeast, barley flour and oil, ground nuts and flour, ground nuts and seeds, wheat flour and egg, wheat flour and yogurt. Some types of pastry are thin and crisp, others thick and spongy. Choose the one that is most useful for your purpose.

Fillings abound in infinite variety and I have given no more than a taste in the pages that follow. Different countries across the world have their own special fillings and pastries. The Greeks and the Arabs use the paper thin filo (phyllo) pastry sheets made with flour and water which have oil or melted butter painted on between them. Chopped nuts are set between the multiple sheets and drenched in a scented syrup. The French *mille feuilles* is a supreme example of puff pastry sandwiched with cream; the Austrians are well-known for their yeast pastries filled with cinnamon and cheese; while the Americans talk about blueberry pie and apple pie in an almost mystical way.

In this book, fresh fruit, dried fruit, beans, vegetables, nuts and spices are all called upon to work their different magic. Any of your favourite fillings can easily be matched with a high-fibre pastry. Carbohydrate and calorie values are given after each pastry recipe and can be simply calculated for each slice. If, for example, you wanted to combine the rough puff pastry which has 100g CHO with your filling of say 60g CHO, the total carbohydrate count would be 160g CHO. If you mark off 16 slices on the pastry each individual slice will equal 10g CHO.

Pastry presents many opportunities for making superb dishes from limited ingredients, but some cooks are unable to exploit this potential because of a pastry phobia. The condition may sound bizarre, but my experience with cookery students has shown there exists a definite psychological block in many minds about making pastry. People are terrified at the thought of it and approach it convinced that it will not work out right. I have even met some home economics teachers and one or two cookery writers who began their careers with pastry anxiety. The main step on the path to successful pastry is to shake off crippling thoughts about not succeeding and to believe that anyone can do it. After that, all that remains is to make the pastry.

The main skills involved are lightness of touch both in binding the dough together and in rolling it out. The important thing to avoid is overworking the pastry. Nervously fiddling with the ingredients makes matters worse instead of better. When you pull the flour, fat and water together into a dough with your hands use large decisive movements, cup your hand so that it is like a massive spoon. Some of my students found this stage physically hard, but we discovered that this can be the result of a lack of flexibility at the wrist. Tilting the bowl to an angle brings the ingredients closer to hand.

Using a food processor or a food mixer does not solve the problem of pastry phobia. It merely puts a wall between yourself and the ingredients. If you use your hands when necessary and allow yourself to respond to the feel and touch of what you are handling, and use your eye to gauge the consistency, you will find that pastry making is a pleasurable experience. And once you are confident about what you are doing, it will become a very quick process. It takes no more than a couple of minutes after the ingredients have been weighed and is quick by hand.

Anything that goes wrong can be rectified. If you add too much liquid and a soggy dough results, add a little extra flour. If the dough feels too dry, you may need a little extra water or fat. Making pastry can be influenced by a number of factors such as how finely the flour is milled, the amount of water in the margarine, the size of the eggs, remembering to use cold water for mixing and bowls that are not hot from washing up. If it does not go exactly as it should there is no need to throw your hands up in despair, but work out for yourself what the problem is and solve it. If the situation is irredeemable you can always start again.

One of the attractions of using pastry is that it is possible to prepare it for the next day if it is wrapped in greaseproof paper and foil and left overnight in the fridge. Remove half an hour before rolling out.

All pastry freezes well. It can be frozen prior to cooking or when baked. Raw pastry keeps for up to one month, cooked pastry for up to three months. Before freezing write a label with details of what the pastry is and if necessary the carbohydrate and calorie content.

Baking tins do not need to be greased unless the recipe specifies this. All the pastry recipes contain some fat or oil and this usually eliminates the need for greasing.

HASTY PASTRY

This is a very quick method of making a crisp wholewheat pastry which is very suitable for tarts or pie crusts. It has a very low fat content.

175g (6 oz) wholewheat flour
2 tbs oil
1 tbs lemon juice
100–125ml (4–4½ fl oz) cold
water

Put the flour in a mixing bowl. Stir in the oil and lemon juice with a knife or wooden spoon. Add just enough water to make thick crumbs which you can work into a soft pastry dough with your hands. This pastry should not be overworked, so do not knead it more than you have to.

Chill in the fridge for half an hour. When rolling it out, sprinkle the board or work top lightly with flour.

Total pastry is 115g CHO. 825 kcals.

YOGURT PASTRY

This is a crisp light pastry which uses very little oil. It has a cakier texture than the other pastries in this section. It should not be baked too long as it can burn easily.

A small 150ml pot of yogurt contains 270mg of calcium, 360mg of potassium, 1mg of zinc and traces of iron and copper. Apart from a high nutritive value, live yogurt contains two bacteria, Streptococcus thermophilus and Lactobacillus bulgarius, both of which are beneficial for digestion of food in the intestine and in consequence for general well-being. These bacteria are only active in live yogurt, so read yogurt labels carefully when shopping: unless specified most are pasteurized. Bulgarian peasants used to consume large amounts of yogurt and their longevity has been linked to this.

150g (5 oz) wholemeal flour
50g (2 oz) soya flour
¼ tsp bicarbonate of soda
2 tbs oil
150ml (5 fl oz) low-fat
   natural yogurt

Combine the flour and bicarbonate of soda in a mixing bowl. Stir in the oil and bind with the yogurt. Work the pastry a little with your hands so that it becomes a light spongy dough. Chill in the fridge for half an hour before use if it has to be rolled thin. Otherwise it can be used immediately.

Total pastry is 120g CHO. 1000 kcals.

SHORT CUT STRUDEL

Crispy thin layers of strudel are a delight to eat and an art to make. It is fascinating to watch experienced pastry cooks working on a strudel pastry using the knuckles of their hands to stretch the dough to a tissue paper consistency. These are skills that most of us working away in our kitchens hoping to achieve maximum results with minimum effort cannot hope to emulate. Nevertheless, we can still make a delicious strudel-type pastry.

Using wholewheat flour in a strudel recipe affects the texture of the pastry and if not worked in the right way it turns out like cardboard. This recipe will not give a pastry as thin as the shop-made kind, but is a speedy route for the average cook to get a strudel-like result. It is fairly quick as the pastry is left to stand for only a short time. Adding oil while rolling it out increases elasticity in the pastry. A delectable strudel can be made without requiring you to learn the skills of generations of Viennese strudel makers!

1 egg, lightly beaten
100g (4 oz) wholewheat flour
3 dessertspoons oil

Combine the egg with the flour and 1 dessertspoon oil in a mixing bowl to make a soft dough. Cover with a thick cloth and leave to stand for 15 minutes.

Roll out the pastry on a clean tablecloth. This stops the pastry sticking and removes any restrictions imposed by the size of the pastry board. Sprinkle the tablecloth with a little flour and roll out the pastry in an oblong shape until it will roll no further. Sprinkle 1 dessertspoon of oil evenly over the surface – rub it lightly across with a pastry brush or your fingers. Now roll out the pastry again, sprinkling a little flour on top so that it does not stick to the rolling pin. (Use a rolling pin without ornate end pieces because they make a ridge on thinly rolled pastry.) The pastry will become thinner.

Lightly sprinkle the remaining dessertspoon of oil over the pastry, again spreading it across the surface. Sprinkle with a little flour and roll out thinly. The pastry should be roughly about 41cm (16 in) square and almost paper thin.

Before filling the pastry lift it onto the baking tray either with your hand or by lifting the tablecloth.

Total strudel pastry is 65g CHO. 480 kcals.

ROUGH PUFF PASTRY

This is a low fat high-fibre version of classic rough puff pastry. The wholewheat flour inhibits the creation of multiple layers of pastry which puff up, but the basic method of layers of fat separating the folds of pastry remains and this creates a supple, easy-to-handle pastry that can be rolled very thin and gives a light crisp result. I find it an invaluable part of my pastry repertoire.

150g (5 oz) wholewheat flour
50g (2 oz) margarine or
    butter
50–75ml (2–3 fl oz) cold
    water

Put the flour in a mixing bowl with the margarine. Cut the margarine into chunks while it is in the flour. Add enough water to bind the flour and margarine into a soft dough.

Place the dough on a lightly floured board or work top and roll it out in a long narrow rectangle about 25×10cm (10×4 in). At this stage lumps of the fat will be visible in the dough. Mark the dough off lightly into three equal sections. Turn the top section over the middle one and fold the third over them both.

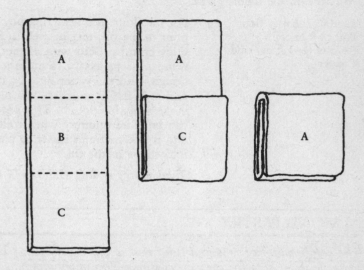

1. Roll out a long narrow rectangle and mark off three equal sections.
2. Fold C over B.
3. Fold A over B and C.

Give the pastry a quarter-turn and repeat this process of rolling out, folding into three and giving a quarter-turn three more times. After completing this the margarine will have been rolled into the flour and the pastry will have an even texture.

Wrap in greaseproof paper and chill in the fridge for 30 minutes. Roll out once more into a rectangle and fold into three before using.

Total pastry is 100g CHO. 850 kcals.

BARLEY PASTRY

Barley flour gives a heavier texture to pastry than wheat flour, but has a nuttier flavour. Barley flour, like wholewheat flour, should be ground from the whole grain.

150g (5 oz) barley flour
50ml (2 fl oz) oil
50–75ml (2–3 fl oz) cold
    water

Put the flour into a mixing bowl and pour in the oil, mixing well to form thick crumbs. Bind with as much water as is necessary to make a soft dough. Add the water little by little, and only use as much as you need to make a pliable dough. This pastry can be quite crumbly when rolled out and it is sometimes easier to pat it into shape in the tin.

Total pastry is 110g CHO. 975 kcals.

ALMOND PASTRY

The combination of nuts and flour makes this a very rich pastry and one to be kept for special occasions. Too many almonds sit heavily on your stomach although a healthy octogenarian of my acquaintance assures me that a few well-chewed almonds without the outer skin give immediate relief from heartburn.

150g (5 oz) wholewheat flour
100g (4 oz) ground almonds
3 tbs oil
1 egg, lightly beaten
25ml (1 fl oz) water

Combine the flour and ground almonds in a mixing bowl. Stir in the oil and egg. Add just enough water to make a pliable dough. Cover and leave in the fridge for one hour before using.

105g CHO. 1520 kcals.

HAZELNUT PASTRY

Hazelnuts were used in many of the cake and confectionery recipes made in late 19th century Vienna, the melting pot of Europe's south-eastern quarter whose inhabitants arrived from the farthest reaches of the Austro-Hungarian Empire.

100g (4 oz) wholewheat flour
100g (4 oz) ground hazelnuts
  (not roasted)
25g (1 oz) butter
1 egg, lightly beaten

Combine the flour and ground hazelnuts in a mixing bowl. Rub in the butter, using your fingertips to make thick crumbs. Add the egg to the mixture to make a dough.

Cover with greaseproof paper and chill in the fridge for 45 minutes before using.

Total pastry is 75g CHO. 955 kcals.

SWEET SEED PASTRY

This is a useful pastry for anyone who needs to avoid flours milled from grains. It is made entirely from ground seeds, nuts and dried figs. All the ingredients in this recipe make their own special nutritional contribution – the seeds in particular are packed with minerals. Pumpkin seeds are rich in iron and contain 15mg per 100g, an amazing 32.5g of protein plus the additional bonus of linoleic unsaturated fatty acids; the sesame seeds are high in calcium containing an impressive 115mg per 100g and are also rich in lecithin; the sunflower seeds provide a calcium booster plus a good supply of magnesium and thiamin, one of the B vitamins. Almonds provide a general mineral pick-me-up including a king-size dose of vitamin E. The figs which bind the seeds and nuts together are high in potassium and fibre.

1 tbs boiling water
50g (2 oz) dried figs, chopped
25g (1 oz) sunflower seeds
25g (1 oz) pumpkin seeds
25g (1 oz) sesame seeds, toasted
25g (1 oz) ground almonds (or ground hazelnuts)
½ tsp mixed spice (cinnamon, cloves and nutmeg)

Pour the boiling water over the figs and leave to stand for 10 minutes. Then purée using an electric coffee grinder (it is particularly suitable for such small amounts).

Grind all the seeds to powder. Combine them in a mixing bowl with the ground almonds and the mixed spice. Bind with the fig paste to make a dough. Sometimes it is necessary to add a little extra water to make the crumbs go into a dough. Chill in the fridge for half an hour before using.

Total pastry is 40g CHO. 675 kcals.

YEAST PASTRY

Yeast pastry is made much faster with vitamin C (ascorbic acid) and yeast than with sugar. The vitamin C removes one of the proving stages in the traditional approach and speeds up the rate at which the dough rises. The first step is to mix the ingredients and knead. The dough is left for a short space of time to rise, long enough to prepare the filling and the baking tray. The second step is to roll out the pastry, fill it and leave it to stand for about 15 minutes before baking.

The nutritional advantage of using yeast pastry is that the leavening process helps the breakdown of phytates which are found in wheat fibre. Phytates can limit the absorption of minerals such as calcium, iron and zinc by the body. If your diet is made up of yeast-based bread with occasional high-fibre biscuits or cakes this will not have any drastic effect, but if you suffer from a deficiency of these minerals then you should avoid unleavened bread and bran-based foods until the shortage has been made up. Many of the fillings in this section can be switched around and used with the yeast pastry.

If you cannot find a 25mg tablet of vitamin C buy the 50mg size and cut it in half. If you halve this recipe use 15g (½ oz) fresh yeast.

400g (14 oz) fine milled
  wholewheat flour
25g (1 oz) fresh yeast
25mg tablet of vitamin C
75g (3 oz) butter or
  margarine
200ml (7 fl oz) water
1 egg

Put the flour into a large mixing bowl. Crumble the yeast and crush the vitamin C tablet into a small bowl. Melt the butter in the water in a small saucepan until the temperature becomes lukewarm. Add a little of this liquid to the yeast and vitamin C to make a creamy mixture. Add the rest of the liquid and stir into the flour. Lightly whisk the egg and add. Work the mixture into a dough with your hands and turn onto a lightly floured board or work top and knead for about 5 minutes, or for about 1 minute in a food processor. Return to the bowl and cover the top with cling film and a clean teatowel and leave to rest for 10 minutes. The pastry is then ready to be rolled out thinly and used.

Total Yeast Pastry is 265g CHO. 1915 kcals.

APPLE AND PEAR PIE WITH CRUMBLE TOPPING

½ quantity of Hasty Pastry
  (see page 86)

Filling
350g (12 oz) eating apples
350g (12 oz) pears
100ml (4 fl oz) water
25g (1 oz) dried apricots,
  chopped

Crumble topping
50g (2 oz) oat bran and germ
50g (2 oz) chopped almonds
2 tbs apple juice,
  unsweetened

Makes 16 small servings

Roll out the pastry thinly and line a 23cm (9 in) diameter pie dish. Bake blind for 10 minutes in a pre-heated oven gas mark 5/190°C/375°F until a pale biscuit colour.

While the pastry is baking prepare the filling. Slice the apples and pears into a saucepan together with the water and apricots. Bring to the boil and simmer for 10 minutes. When the pastry is cooked, pour the fruit and its juice into the pastry-lined dish.

Prepare the topping: combine the oat bran and germ and almonds with the apple juice to make thick crumbs. Sprinkle this over the top of the fruit.

Bake in a preheated oven gas mark 4/ 180°C/350°F for 15–20 minutes until it is browned all over.

Each serving is 10g CHO. 75 kcals.

APPLE AND ADUKI PIE

This may sound an improbable combination, but the result is very pleasant tasting and light on the stomach. It is a modified version of a macrobiotic recipe – the original would have rather more aduki beans and omit the few sultanas. The aduki bean and the juice it is cooked in is held in particularly high regard by macrobiotics; it is meant to be beneficial for the kidneys and less gaseous than other beans. The Japanese, whose cuisine seems to be the basis for many macrobiotic dishes, are also fond of this bean and use it for sweets and jelly, as well as cooked with rice. According to Lesley Downer, a writer on Japanese cuisine, aduki bean paste, which forms the basis for many of these dishes, used to be made unsweetened, with just a pinch of salt to bring out the natural sweetness. Today the bean paste is sweetened with sugar.

Aduki beans contain about 25 per cent protein, some iron, calcium and some of the B vitamins.

Filling
100g (4 oz) dried aduki beans
25g (1 oz) sultanas
350g (12 oz) eating apples
1 tsp cinnamon

1 quantity of Hasty Pastry
 (see page 86)

Makes 10 large servings

Prepare the filling. Soak the aduki beans in cold water overnight. Cook in a pressure cooker or saucepan until they are soft and moist. Before using in the pie, boil away most of the cooking liquid, but not so much that the beans dry out. Soak the sultanas in a little water for 30 minutes.

Roll out the pastry thinly. Use a 20cm (8 in) diameter pie dish to cut out 2 circles. The pastry base should be slightly larger than the top so that it covers the sides of the dish.

Pour the cold aduki beans evenly over the bottom of the pie. Place the sultanas at equal intervals over the beans and sprinkle the surface with ½ tsp cinnamon. Slice the apples thinly over the surface of the beans. Sprinkle with the remaining ½ tsp cinnamon. Lay the pastry lid on top and pinch the sides of the pie together.

Bake in a preheated oven gas mark 5/ 190°C/375°F for 30–40 minutes until the pastry is evenly browned.

Each serving is 20g CHO. 130 kcals.

MANGO PIE DELIGHT

This recipe is based on the traditional English approach to pies, of combining a fruit filling on a pastry base with a layer of meringue on top, but by using an exotic fruit the mundane is transformed into something quite mouthwatering. The puréed fruit looks like a creamy custard, waiting to ooze out with each mouthful.

½ quantity of Yogurt Pastry
  (see page 86–7)

Filling
1 small mango (weighing
  about 300g/11 oz)
1 eating apple (weighing
  about 125g/4½ oz)
2 tbs apple juice
1 egg yolk

Topping
1 egg white
25g (1 oz) ripe banana,
  peeled

Makes 6 large slices

Roll out the pastry and line a (17.5cm/7 in) baking dish. Bake blind for 10 minutes in a preheated oven gas mark 5/190°C/375°F.

While the pastry is baking prepare the filling. Peel the mango and slice the flesh. Slice the apple into the blender and add the mango and apple juice. Blend to make a thick purée. Add the egg yolk and blend for a few seconds more. Pour into the partly cooked pastry case and bake for 12–15 minutes in a slightly cooler oven gas mark 4/180°C/350°F.

While the fruit filling is cooking prepare the topping. Whisk the egg white stiffly. Mouli or sieve the banana and fold in with a metal spoon. Spoon thinly over the top of the fruit and return to a cooler oven gas mark 3/170°C/325°F for about 10 minutes until it is lightly browned. Serve hot or cold.

Each slice is 20g CHO. 140 kcals.

APPLE STRUDEL

We used to be taught, 'An apple a day keeps the doctor away', but the lesson seems to have been forgotten. Despite the availability of an ever increasing number of varieties such as Discovery and Jonathan in the shops – or perhaps because of the confusion bred by this profusion – UK consumption has fallen to around one large apple per person a week. This strudel may help whet your appetite for larger doses of the fruit of paradise.

1 quantity of Strudel Pastry (see page 87–8)

Filling
400g (14 oz) eating apples, peeled and chopped
25g (1 oz) sultanas
25g (1 oz) raisins
50g (2 oz) almonds, chopped
½–1 tsp cinnamon
½ tsp mixed spice
zest of ½ lemon
2 tbs orange juice, unsweetened
1 dessertspoon oil

Makes 12 slices

Preheat the oven to gas mark 4/ 180°C/350°F. Lay the strudel pastry over a large baking tray so that it is ready for filling. This avoids having to lift it after filling.

Prepare the filling: mix the apples with the sultanas and raisins in a large bowl. Add the chopped almonds, spices, lemon zest and orange juice. Spoon this mixture along the entire length of the strudel leaving a margin of 4cm (1½ in) at each end.

Lightly fold one side of the pastry over the fruit and then fold the other side to overlap it on top. This makes an oblong shape. Brush a little oil on one of the sides to help them stick together. Seal the two ends of the strudel.

Put a dessertspoon of oil in the bowl that the apple mixture stood in. Mix it up with the spices that are around the sides of the bowl and dribble the spiced oil along the top of the strudel. A little more cinnamon can be sprinkled on top according to taste.

Bake for 40–45 minutes until the pastry is browned and crisp.

Each slice is 10g CHO. 85 kcals.

PECAN PIE

Pecan nuts are grown in the southern states of the USA and pecan pie is an American invention. The pecan, a very sweet tasting nut, is a good source of potassium, magnesium, iron and zinc and, unusually for nuts, contains a small amount of vitamin C.

Filling
100g (4 oz) prunes, stoned
    and chopped
100ml (4 fl oz) water
150g (5 oz) pecan nuts
250g (9 oz) firm tofu
100g (4 oz) banana, peeled
1 egg, lightly beaten
25g (1 oz) oatmeal (or
    porridge oats ground to a
    fine flour)
a few drops of vanilla essence
½ tsp cinnamon

½ quantity of Rough Puff
    Pastry (see page 88–9)

Makes 12 servings

Soak the prunes in the water for 15 minutes.

Roll out the pastry in a square so that it will cover the base of a 20cm (8 in) square baking dish. Bake blind in a preheated oven gas mark 4/ 180°C/350°F for 10 minutes.

Prepare the filling: pour the prunes and water into a small saucepan and cook on a low heat until the water is absorbed and a thick paste is formed. Blend in the liquidizer if the paste looks too coarse.

Grind the pecan nuts and combine with the moulied tofu. The texture will be thick and a little coarse. Add the prune paste, mashed banana, egg, oatmeal, vanilla essence and cinnamon. (If using a food processor blend the prunes, nuts and tofu together.)

Spread the mixture as evenly as possible over the partly baked pastry shell. Bake in a preheated oven gas mark 4/180°C/350°F for 20 minutes until the filling has set firmly. Serve cold.

Each serving is 10g CHO. 160 kcals.

ORANGE CAROB PIE

Recent research in the USA has linked the three minerals magnesium, potassium and calcium with a reduction in blood pressure levels. The research suggests that magnesium helps protect against the development of high blood pressure in old age, while calcium and potassium have been most effective in counter-balancing high blood pressure in people who are salt-sensitive. In this recipe the seeds in the pastry are a source of magnesium and potassium while yogurt is a good source of calcium.

1 quantity of Sweet Seed Pastry (see page 91–2)

Filling
225g (8 oz) firm tofu
100g (4 oz) banana
50g (2 oz) carob powder
150ml (5 fl oz) low-fat natural yogurt
1 egg
2 medium oranges, weighing about 300g (11 oz)

Makes 10 servings

Press the pastry over the base of a 23cm (9 in) baking dish. Bake in a preheated oven gas mark 4/180°C/350°F for 10 minutes.

Prepare the filling: use a liquidizer or food processor to blend the tofu and banana to a smooth cream. Add the carob, yogurt and lightly beaten egg.

Peel the oranges and remove the pith and seeds. Chop into small pieces and add them, together with any juice, into the tofu-carob mixture and stir gently. Pour into the pastry shell. The mixture has a thick custard-like texture.

Return to the oven for 30–35 minutes and bake until the tofu mixture is firmly set.

Each serving is 10g CHO. 120 kcals.

PEACH CUSTARD TART

Scrumptious slices of peach are set in a fruit custard on a thick cakey pastry base. The combination of fruit in this recipe makes it superbly sweet and useful to make when still trying to get used to doing without sugar.

Custard
50g (2 oz) dried apricots
50ml (2 fl oz) boiling water
1 egg
150ml (5 fl oz) low-fat
  natural yogurt
50g (2 oz) ground almonds

1 quantity of Yogurt Pastry
  (see page 86-7)

Fruit filling
200g (7 oz) pears
2 tbs apple juice

Topping
400g (14 oz) firm ripe
  peaches

Makes 10 slices

Pour the boiling water over the dried apricots for the custard and leave to stand.

Prepare the pastry: there is no need to chill it before using. Roll it out thickly and line a 25cm (10 in) diameter baking dish. Cut off any surplus pastry around the sides. Bake blind in a preheated oven gas mark 5/190°C/375°F for 10 minutes until a light biscuit colour.

While the pastry is baking, prepare the fruit filling. Blend the pears and apple juice and put to one side.

Prepare the custard: grind the dried apricots with their soaking water to a paste, using a hand grinder or electric coffee grinder. Whisk the egg and fold in the yogurt, ground apricots and almonds.

Take the pastry out of the oven. Spread the pear purée thinly and evenly over the base. Spoon the custard on top. Return to a slightly cooler oven gas mark 4/180°C/350°F for 20-25 minutes until the custard is firm. By the time the custard is set the sides of the pastry will be brown but not burnt.

While the custard is baking prepare the topping. Pour boiling water over the peaches and leave for 15 seconds then remove the skins. Cut into thin, even slices. When the custard is firm and the tart has been removed from the oven, lay the peaches in circles around the top, completely covering the custard. Return to the oven and bake for a further 5 minutes.

Each slice is 20g CHO. 175 kcals.

STRAWBERRY TART

Strawberries are set in jelly on a crisp thin pastry base in this tart, which tastes best if eaten the same day it is made.

½ quantity of Rough Puff
Pastry (see page 88–9)

Filling
25g (1 oz) ground almonds
500g (1lb 2 oz) fresh
strawberries, hulled
125ml (4½ fl oz) apple juice,
unsweetened
25ml (1 fl oz) water
½ level tsp agar-agar powder

Makes 8 servings

Roll out the pastry thinly to fit a circular 20cm (8 in) diameter pastry dish. Bake blind in a preheated oven gas mark 5/190°C/375°F for 20–25 minutes until crisp and browned. Remove from the oven and leave to cool.

Prepare the filling: cover the base of the pastry with the ground almonds.

Cut the strawberries in half and place them flat side down around the pastry base, making two layers of fruit.

Combine the apple juice and water and dissolve the agar-agar powder in the liquid. Pour into a small pan and bring to the boil for 1½ minutes. Remove from the heat and allow to cool for a few minutes. Pour evenly over the fruit.

Each serving is 10g CHO. 95 kcals.

FRUIT TARTS

These rough puff pastry tarts are filled with cherries, but this recipe works just as well with whatever fruit is in season. A midsummer combination of raspberries, blackcurrants and strawberries looks very eyecatching. For midwinter thin slices of banana and grapes set in a layer of jelly work equally well. The tarts are fairly quick to make although stoning cherries can be laborious work – soft fruits are much quicker to prepare. These tarts look their best if eaten the same day, but still taste fine if eaten the day after.

1 quantity of Rough Puff
   Pastry (see page 88–9)

Filling
700g (1lb 9 oz) black cherries
30g (1 oz generous) ground
   almonds
½ tsp cinnamon

Jelly
150ml + 1 tbs (5 fl oz +
   1 tbs) apple juice,
   unsweetened
50ml + 1 tbs (2 fl oz +
   1 tbs) water
½ generous tsp agar-agar
   powder

Makes 24 tarts

Roll out the pastry thinly enough to cut 24 circles 7.5cm (3 in) in diameter. Press the circles into tart tins and bake blind in a preheated oven gas mark 5/190°C/375°F for 15 minutes until crisp and browned.

Prepare the filling: remove the stones from the cherries. Try and keep them whole because this looks more attractive than pieces.

Combine the ground almonds and cinnamon. Spoon out a little into the base of each tart. Place enough cherries in each one so that they look full.

Prepare the jelly: combine the apple juice and water in a small saucepan. Take 1 tbs of this liquid and mix with the agar-agar powder then pour it back into the saucepan. Bring to the boil and simmer for 1½ minutes. The jelly will take about 7–10 minutes to set. Leave it to cool for a few minutes. When cool put 2 tsp in each tart. With practice you will be able to gauge when the jelly is a few minutes from setting. The reason for waiting is that if you put boiling liquid jelly into a pastry case it will soften it and make it soggy. If you wait a little you will keep the contrast of a soft filling with a crisp outside.

Each tart is 10g CHO. 55 kcals.

CAROB CREAM TART

This is a very elegant tart. The combination of crisp pastry and firm carob mousse filling makes it a sensational but delicate dessert.

1 quantity of Rough Puff Pastry (see page 88–9)

Filling
200g (7 oz) firm tofu
200g (7 oz) ripe bananas, peeled
½ tsp vanilla essence
4 tbs orange juice
1 tbs brandy (optional)
100g (4 oz) carob powder
200ml (7 fl oz) skimmed milk
200ml (7 fl oz) water
1 tbs agar-agar flakes or 2 tsp agar powder
2 egg whites, stiffly beaten

Makes 20 slices

Roll out the pastry thinly to cover the base and a little of the sides of a 30×20cm (12×8 in) baking tin. Bake blind in a preheated oven gas mark 5/190°C/375°F for 10–15 minutes until evenly browned, but be careful that it does not burn.

While the pastry is cooling prepare the filling. Use a food processor or food mill to blend the tofu and banana. Add the vanilla essence, orange juice and brandy. In a small saucepan combine the carob powder, milk, water and agar-agar flakes. Bring to the boil and simmer on a low heat for 5 minutes stirring all the time and making sure the mixture does not become too thick. If using agar-agar powder dissolve in a dessertspoon of water and add to the carob, milk and water in the saucepan after they have cooked gently for 3 minutes. Let the agar-agar solution simmer for a further 2 minutes.

Take the saucepan off the heat and add to the blended tofu-banana mixture. Fold in the egg whites and pour the mixture evenly over the pastry shell. Agar-agar does not require refrigeration to set and will become firm quite quickly. Chill the tart before serving.

Each slice is 10g CHO. 90 kcals.

APRICOT TART

Dried apricots have a very rich taste which always dominates whatever recipe they are used in. Many people prefer the strong taste of the dried variety to fresh ones. The vivid-coloured apricots are usually coated in sulphur, E220, in order to preserve that bright shade. Unsulphured apricots are available from wholefood shops although, of course, once additive-free the colour is a dark brown.

Dieters can bake the filling without the pastry.

Filling
400g (14 oz) dried apricots
400ml (14 fl oz) water
200g (7 oz) firm tofu
100ml (4 fl oz) apple juice, unsweetened

1 quantity of Barley Pastry (see page 90)

Makes 16 slices

Soak the apricots in the water overnight. Put the apricots and soaking water in a saucepan and simmer on a low heat until the water has been absorbed. Leave to cool.

Remove and reserve a dessertspoon of the pastry then either roll or pat out the remainder to fit a 23cm (9 in) diameter baking tin. Bake in a preheated oven gas mark 4/ 180°C/350°F for 15–20 minutes until lightly browned.

Prepare the filling: blend the softened apricots, tofu and apple juice to make a stiff paste. Spread it evenly over the partly-cooked pastry base.

Take a small piece of reserved pastry and make into little balls. Flatten between your fingers to form circles about 3cm (1¼ in) in diameter. Dot these over the top of the apricot filling. Return to a slightly warmer oven gas mark 5/190°C/375°F for 15 minutes until the apricot has set and the pastry is brown at the edges.

Each slice is 20g CHO. 115 kcals.

FRUTTI ALMOND TART

This is a rich concoction of softened winter fruit in layers of crisp Almond Pastry. This pastry keeps very well for at least 24 hours if it is stored in a tin after baking and cooling, so it can be prepared in advance and the filling completed later.

1 quantity of Almond Pastry
  (see page 90)
1 egg white
25g (1 oz) ground almonds

Filling
275g (10 oz) pears
325g (11½ oz) eating apples
275g (10 oz) satsumas, peeled
75g (3 oz) banana, peeled
100ml (4 fl oz) apple juice
pinch of cinnamon

Makes 10 servings

Divide the pastry into three equal pieces and roll out each one into a circle. Use an upturned 23cm (9 in) bowl to cut the circles. If the pastry is difficult to handle place it on a 23cm (9 in) baking dish which is covered with a sheet of greaseproof paper and use it as a mould. Press gently with your fingers so that the pastry fills the base of the dish. When you have the complete circular shape, lift up the greaseproof paper with the pastry on and place it on a baking tray. Repeat this process for the other two circles.

Whisk the egg white to stiff peaks. Choosing the pastry circle that looks the best spread the egg white over the top and then sprinkle ground almonds over the surface. This makes a very effective topping.

Bake the circles in a preheated oven gas mark 4/180°C/350°F for 15–20 minutes until the pastry is evenly browned. Make sure the circles do not start to burn at the edges. Remove from the baking trays when cool.

Prepare the filling: chop the fruit into medium-sized pieces and put in a heavy saucepan with the fruit juice and cinnamon. Cook over a low heat for about 10 minutes until the fruit is softened but not mushy. If there is too much liquid boil it down after removing the fruit with a slotted spoon.

When the filling is cool assemble the tart. Spread half the filling on one pastry circle. Place the second circle on top. Spread the remaining filling evenly across its surface. Place the third circle with the meringue and nuts on top to crown the tart.

Each portion is 20g CHO. 205 kcals.

ICE CREAM TORTE

This is definitely a special occasion cake. It has to be eaten on the same day so be sure you have a lot of people to help you! As the velvety ice cream is made with tofu rather than cream it is a very light cake.

Another attraction of this torte is that it can be prepared in advance and so reduce pressure on the cook. If you bake the pastry the day before it is needed then you only have to make the ice cream on the day.

1 quantity of Almond Pastry
  (see page 90)
1 quantity of Almond Carob
  Ice Cream (see page 174–5)
flaked almonds
a few strawberries or kiwi
  fruit

Makes 8 large servings

Divide the pastry into three equal pieces and roll out each one into a circle. Use an upturned 23cm (9 in) bowl to cut the circle. If the pastry is difficult to handle place it on a 23cm (9 in) baking dish which is covered with a sheet of greaseproof paper and use it as a mould. Press gently with your fingers so that the pastry fills the base of the dish. When you have the complete circular shape, lift up the greaseproof paper with the pastry on and place it on the baking tray. Repeat this process for the other two circles.

Bake in a preheated oven gas mark 4/ 180°C/350°F for 20 minutes until the pastry is evenly browned. It should not be too brown, but it should be crisp when you eat it. Remove from the baking trays when cool. Store in a tin if they are to be used the next day.

Prepare the ice cream and store in the fridge until you are ready to put the torte together. Spread each circle of pastry with ice cream and put the layers on top of each other to give a three-tier torte, with the top layer also covered in ice cream. Sprinkle it with a few flaked almonds and decorate the sides with halved strawberries or slices of kiwi fruit.

Each serving is 20g CHO. 225 kcals.

BANANA AND ALMOND ROLL

Bananas and almonds are an unusual combination of flavours, but they work very well together in this rough puff pastry roll. It is satisfyingly filling and can be served in thin slices or large chunks. It tastes just as good the day after it is baked and also freezes well.

Filling
200g (7 oz) firm tofu
400g (14 oz) ripe bananas
100g (4 oz) ground almonds
½ tsp almond essence

1 quantity of Rough Puff
  Pastry (see page 88–9)

Makes 16 slices

Prepare the filling: use a food processor or food mill to blend the tofu and bananas. Add the ground almonds and almond essence. The filling is very firm and holds its shape during baking.

Roll out the pastry to roughly 30×40cm (12×16 in), but make sure that you have not rolled it so thin that it tears. Cut it in half so that each piece is about 30×20cm (12×8 in).

Divide the filling in half and spread one half over one of the pieces of pastry, leaving a margin of 2.5cm (1 in) all the way round. Gently roll up the pastry and seal the ends firmly, otherwise the filling will ooze out during baking. Mark off 8 slices along the length of the roll. Make another roll with the remaining piece of pastry and the rest of the filling. Transfer carefully to an ungreased baking tray. Bake in a preheated oven gas mark 5/190°C/375°F for 35–40 minutes until lightly browned and the pastry is cooked all the way through.

Serving suggestion: if you serve this roll as a dessert cut each roll into 16 slices and serve each one with a slice of kiwi fruit on top.

Each slice is 10g CHO. 115 kcals.

CAROB ROLL

Thin Rough Puff Pastry spread with a creamy carob filling and made into a long roll makes a delicious pastry for the tea table.

Filling
100g (4 oz) raisins
100ml (4 fl oz) water
200g (7 oz) firm tofu
40g (1½ oz) carob powder
50ml (2 fl oz) orange juice, unsweetened

½ quantity Rough Puff Pastry (see page 88–9)

Makes 12 slices

Prepare the filling: put the raisins and water in a small saucepan and simmer until all the water is absorbed. Blend to a paste in an electric coffee grinder.

Use a food processor or food mill to blend the tofu. Add the carob powder, orange juice and raisin paste.

Roll out the pastry to roughly 20×30cm (8×12 in), but make sure there are no holes in the surface because the filling will leak out during baking. Spread the filling evenly over the surface of the pastry, leaving a margin of 2.5cm (1 in) all the way round. Roll up the pastry loosely and seal firmly at each end and underneath. Transfer carefully to an ungreased baking tray.

Bake in a preheated oven gas mark 5/ 190°C/375°F for 35–40 minutes until the top is lightly browned and the pastry is cooked all the way through.

Each slice is 10g CHO. 75 kcals.

WALNUT CRESCENTS

Walnuts are loaded with nutrients. They contain protein, potassium, magnesium, calcium, iron and as much zinc as a tin of sardines. Zinc is said by some researchers to be beneficial for fertility, foetal growth and acne. Post-natal depression is also linked by some doctors with zinc deficiency.

When you eat a walnut you get a mineral and vitamin package made by nature, while if you dose yourself with supplements of different minerals it is quite likely that essential nutritive elements and balances that can only be found in foods are being omitted.

Filling
50g (2 oz) dried dates, chopped
50ml (2 fl oz) water
200mg (7 oz) walnuts, chopped
½ tsp cinnamon

1 quantity of Yogurt Pastry (see page 000)

Makes 32 crescents

Prepare the filling: heat the dates and water in a small saucepan until all the water is absorbed and a paste is formed. Leave to cool. Add the chopped walnuts and cinnamon to make a thick crunchy mixture.

Roll out the pastry thinly and cut 32 circles 7.5cm (3 in) in diameter. Place an equal amount of filling on each one. Bring the two sides over to meet in the middle and pinch together to make a standing half-circle or crescent. Place on an ungreased baking tray.

Bake in a preheated oven gas mark 4/180°C/350°F for 20 minutes until lightly browned. Serve hot or cold.

2 crescents are 10g CHO. 135 kcals.

STRAWBERRY HATS

Crisp circles of sweet Hazelnut Pastry are sandwiched together over plump strawberries sitting in a bed of fromage frais.

1 quantity of Hazelnut Pastry (see page 91)

Filling
300g (11 oz) strawberries, hulled
150ml (5 fl oz) fromage frais

Makes 8 Strawberry Hats

Roll out the pastry thinly on a lightly floured board and cut 16 circles 7.5cm (3 in) in diameter. Place on a greased baking tray and bake in a preheated oven gas mark 4/170°C/350°F for 15–20 minutes until lightly browned.

When cool, take eight of the circles and lay them on a flat plate. Put a generous teaspoon of fromage frais on each one. Place about 3 whole strawberries on each portion of fromage frais. On each of the remaining eight pastry circles put a teaspoon of fromage frais and place each one this side down on top of the strawberries so that they are sandwiched with the cheese top and bottom.

Each hat is 10g CHO. 140 kcals.

CINNAMON ROLL

Filling
200g (7 oz) raisins, chopped
  coarsely
250ml (9 fl oz) water
5 tsp cinnamon
100g (4 oz) ground almonds
50g (2 oz) flaked almonds
100ml (4 oz) orange juice,
  freshly squeezed
a little beaten egg mixed with
  1 tsp water (for
  decoration)
cinnamon (for decoration)

½ quantity of Yeast Pastry
  (see page 92–3)
Coconut Icing (optional) (see
  page 57)

Makes 24 slices, 12 in each
  roll.

Prepare the filling: soak the raisins in
the water for half an hour. Put the
raisins and soaking water in a small
saucepan and heat gently until most
of the water has been absorbed.
Leave to cool. Combine the
cinnamon, ground and flaked
almonds in a mixing bowl. Add the
raisins, the leftover cooking juice and
the orange juice. Mix to form a thick
paste.

Divide the pastry in half and roll out
each piece into a large thin rectangle.

Lay one of the pieces of pastry on a
lightly greased baking tray. Spread
half the filling over the pastry. Roll it
up tightly and seal the ends. Repeat
this process for the second piece of
pastry.

Cover the rolls loosely with cling film
and leave to stand in a warm room
for 20 minutes while they increase in
bulk. Brush with the egg and water.
Sprinkle the cinnamon over the top.

Bake in a preheated oven gas mark
5/ 190°C/375°F for 30 minutes until
the pastry is browned. Avoid
overcooking or the roll will taste dry.

Make a little coconut icing (see page
57) and pour over the top (optional).

Each slice is 10g CHO. 100 kcals.

APRICOT RING

Filling
200ml (7 fl oz) water
225g (8 oz) dried apricots
200g (7 oz) sesame seeds
50g (2 oz) ground almonds
50g (2 oz) wheatgerm
2 tbs lemon juice
200ml (7 fl oz) skimmed milk

½ quantity of Yeast Pastry
(see page 92–3)

Icing
50g (2 oz) coconut cream
100ml (4 fl oz) water
½ tsp vanilla essence
½ tsp cinnamon
3 large dried apricots,
weighing about 20g (¾
oz), chopped

Makes 24 slices

Prepare the filling: boil the water and soak the apricots in it for an hour. Chop the apricots and simmer in a small saucepan with the soaking liquid until all the water is absorbed. Leave to cool and prepare the pastry.

Lightly brown the sesame seeds under the grill. Combine them with the chopped apricots, ground almonds, wheatgerm, lemon juice and milk.

Roll out the pastry thinly into a large rectangle, about 60×30cm (24×12 in). This is big enough to roll up into a ring after it has been filled, sealing the two ends together. If this size is too large for your pastry board or work top, roll out the pastry on a clean tablecloth on the kitchen table.

Spread the filling thinly over as much of the pastry surface as possible. Roll up swiss roll fashion, with the seam underneath. Join the ends and place on a lightly greased baking tray. Cover loosely with cling film and leave to stand in a warm room for 20 minutes until the bulk has increased. Bake in a preheated oven gas mark 5/190°C/375°F for 30–35 minutes until well browned.

Prepare the icing: chop up the coconut cream and heat in a small saucepan with the water. When it forms a thick paste add the vanilla essence and cinnamon. Spread over the top of the roll. Decorate the icing with the chopped apricots.

Each slice is 10g CHO. 135 kcals.

8 FRUIT DESSERTS

Fruit desserts depend on the quality of the fresh fruit you use. A favourite market stall or a fruitful relationship with your local greengrocer is essential. There is no reincarnation for sad and old bruised fruit by plunging them into the hopeful disguise of a fruit salad. It will only ruin the taste of the good fruit you use.

You may need to play the detective to find out the days your greengrocer goes to market. If you grow fruit in your own garden then no one can match you for freshness.

These recipes are all quick to make and look attractive.

CLEMENTINE CREAM DELIGHT

The ever-ready packet of tofu in your fridge can be called to service yet again in this dessert of segments of sweet clementine coated with a delicate-tasting orange cream. Prepare it at least four hours in advance as it improves with standing in the fridge while the tofu absorbs the fruit flavours. Either serve it by itself or with a light cake such as Walnut Cake (see page 152–3).

Clementines have a skin that is easily removed and are a sweet juicy fruit. Usually they can only be bought in the winter months. When choosing clementines pick the heaviest ones as these are the juiciest.

175g (6 oz) firm tofu
juice and zest of 1 large
    orange, weighing about
    250g (9 oz)
450g (1 lb) sweet clementines
1 heaped tsp desiccated
    coconut, unsweetened

Makes 4 servings

Pour off the liquid from the tofu packet and either mouli or blend the tofu in a food processor to make a thick cream.

Squeeze the juice out of both halves of the orange and grate the zest. Add the orange juice and zest to the tofu to make it into a creamy liquid.

Peel the clementines and remove the white pith around the segments before adding them to the bowl of creamy tofu. Stir together and lightly sprinkle the top with coconut. Chill in the fridge for at least 4 hours before serving.

Each serving is 10g CHO. 75 kcals.

DATE DELIGHT

When succulent fresh dates are available use them for this quick, light dessert.

200g (7 oz) fresh dates, with stones
100g (4 oz) almond flakes
1 pear, grated
a couple of mint leaves, for decoration

Makes 6 small servings

Remove the stones from the dates and chop the fruit into small pieces with a knife. Combine with the flaked almonds and grated pear. Spoon into a shallow serving bowl and leave to chill in the fridge for one hour before serving. Decorate with a couple of mint leaves.

An alternate way of serving Date Delight is to spoon the mixture into paper cases.

Each portion is 10g CHO. 130 kcals.

POMEGRANATE DIP

Pomegranates have become more available in the last few years and can be found in street markets as well as in the shops. When buying this fruit avoid those whose hard skin has split open. Look for a pinkish glowing skin, with deeper shades of red. If it is too pale the seeds will not be sweet enough, while if it is too red the seeds may be over-ripe with an unpleasant tang.

Pomegranates are high in potassium and chloride. The ancient Greeks and Romans used them for medicinal purposes. Today in parts of India the rind is used against chronic dysentery.

One of the simplest and most enjoyable ways to eat pomegranate is to cut the whole fruit, including the rind, into quarters. In this recipe the seeds are removed from the rind and placed in a large bowl – all your guests have to do is eat them.

2 large pomegranates
50g (2 oz) almonds, with
  skins
2 medium-sized eating
  apples, weighing about
  250g (9 oz)

Makes 4 servings

Remove the pomegranate seeds from the rind and put them in an attractive serving bowl. Keep back 1 tablespoonful and put in a glass. Crush these with the back of a spoon so that the juice runs out. Pour back into the bowl. Chop the almonds into chunky pieces and add.

Just before serving thinly slice the apples into rounds and put on a separate plate. Guests serve themselves by spooning the pomegranate onto a slice of apple.

This is a very sociable dessert!

Each serving is 15g CHO. 120 kcals.

FIGS AU FROMAGE FRAIS

This dish takes one minute to prepare. It is so delicious that you feel like throwing all caution to the wind and gorging yourself. The recipe uses dried figs because they are available all year round at considerably less cost than fresh figs. Having lived abroad and bought figs by the kilo in the local market I always find it painful to pay the equivalent price for one fresh fig. But if you can track down a shop or market stall that is not too expensive, then do use them in this recipe.

Fromage frais has a light creamy taste. The amount of fat in the low-fat-version differs according to the manufacturer.

100g (4 oz) dried figs or
  5 fresh figs
300g (11 oz) fromage frais

Makes 4 small servings

Chop the figs into smallish pieces. Combine in a bowl with the fromage frais. Leave to chill in the fridge for ½–2 hours before serving.

Each portion is 15g CHO. 85 kcals.

JULY FRUIT SALAD

*This fruit salad uses fruit that is readily available in the shops
during July.*

*We first ate this salad with a friend who lives in a tiny house
with one room on each floor. It is opposite an Italian restaurant
with only a narrow walkway between the two buildings. As it was
a hot balmy July evening the restaurant tables had spilled out into
the street almost up to our friend's front door. The room where we
ate was on the first floor and opposite us on the restaurant balcony
people stood drinking while waiting for a free table. While
contemplating Italian culinary delights they couldn't keep their eyes
off us devouring this delicious fruit salad, and were probably
wishing their turn to eat would come quickly.*

juice of 1 large orange, about
    150ml (5 fl oz)
1 tbs cognac (optional)
1 nectarine
1 peach
1 pear
50g (2 oz) banana, peeled
300g (11 oz) galia or
    charantais melon without
    seeds
100g (4 oz) dark red cherries
100g (4 oz) strawberries,
    hulled

Makes 4 large servings

Pour the orange juice into a fruit
salad bowl and mix with the cognac.

Chop the nectarine, peach and pear
flesh into small cubes and put into
the juice. Slice the banana very thinly
and add. Scoop the melon into balls,
using a special cutter or a small
teaspoon. Slice and stone the cherries
and add. Turn the fruit over a few
times with a large spoon so that it
has all been soaked in the juice.
Decorate the top with slices of
strawberry. Leave to stand in the
fridge for 1–2 hours before serving.

Each serving is 20g CHO. 90 kcals.

MELON BOWLS

*Apart from being juicy and sweet this dish is aesthetically pleasing.
It is a subtle blend of different shades of green. A matching
tablecloth and bowls will make it look spectacular.*

*The kiwi fruit is thought of as being typically antipodean, but it
originates from the Yangtze valley in China. In about 1900 a
British botanist collected samples of a few plants in China and*

brought them to the West. The kiwi was one of these and was first grown in New Zealand in 1906. It is rich in vitamin C.

1 large ripe galia melon
   weighing about 1.5–1.7kg
   (3lb 5 oz–3lb 12 oz)
200g (7 oz) seedless grapes
3 kiwi fruit

Makes 6 servings

Cut the melon in half. The shells will be used as bowls for the fruit so when you cut the melon off the rind leave about 1.5cm (¾ in) thickness all the way round, otherwise the rind will not be thick enough.

Scoop the melon flesh into balls using a special cutter or small teaspoon. Put all the balls in a large fruit salad bowl. Add the grapes. Slice the kiwi fruit thinly and add. There should be rather a lot of juice in the bowl from the ripe melon. Pour this into a small saucepan and bring to the boil until the liquid is reduced by half. Leave to cool then pour over the fruit. Chill in the fridge. Just before serving, spoon the fruit into the two melon shells.

Each serving is 15g CHO. 65 kcals.

WILD HIMALAYAN APRICOTS IN ROSEWATER

This item appeared on the menu of a favourite Indian vegetarian restaurant. Images of Himalayan hunters hot in the pursuit of savage apricots flashed across my mind – it was a dish I had to order. When the bowl was set in front of me, I realized that the strange hard brown nuts labelled as Hunza apricots I had half-noticed in my local health food shop were the very same Himalayan apricots.

The Hunzas live in the foothills of the Himalayas and apricots form an important part of their mostly vegetarian diet. They eat them fresh in season and sun-dried out of season. Sir Robert McCarrison, in his studies of diet in India early this century, writes about the Hunzas' good health and 'freedom from disease in general'.

The seed inside the apricots can be cracked and a delectable-tasting almond-shaped nut is found inside.

225g (8 oz) Hunza apricots
500ml (15 fl oz) spring water
1 tbs rosewater to taste

Makes 4 servings

Wash the apricots and place them in an attractive bowl. Pour the water and rosewater over them. Leave them to stand covered overnight in the fridge. In the morning they will have swollen up and become soft. If there is not enough juice add more water and taste to see if further rosewater is necessary.

Each serving is 20g CHO. 90 kcals.

CHILLED ALMOND GLOBES IN PASTEL PINK SAUCE

This unusual dessert requires no cooking and can be prepared in advance. The almond globes are quite substantial and go very well with the fruit sauce. This is a very nutritious dish as the tofu and almonds are both high in protein while the fruit sauce adds an injection of vitamin C.

Almond globes
150g (5 oz) firm tofu
150g (5 oz) ground almonds
75g (3 oz) ripe banana,
    mashed
3 tsp rosewater

1 quantity of Pastel Pink
    Sauce (see page 156)

Makes 6 servings

Make the almond globes by using a food processor or by hand. If using a processor put all the ingredients in the mixing bowl and process until a thick paste is formed. If doing this by hand mash the tofu with a fork and continue to mash it as you work in the ground almonds, mashed banana and rosewater. Gradually a thick paste is formed.

Use an ice-cream scoop to make six rounds. Put them in a freezer container with a lid and place them at the bottom of the freezer for about an hour or so that they become very chilled but not frozen.

Use six small plates for serving. Spoon the sauce over each plate and place a chilled globe in the centre.

Each serving is 10g CHO. 190 kcals.

PEACH MILLET DELIGHT

This is a simple nutritious dish. Millet is not widely used in Europe, but is a staple in parts of India and Africa where it has been cultivated for 6000 years. In Britain the chief consumers are budgies – which seems a pity. Millet is a gluten-free cereal.

The nutritional value of millet changes depending on the variety, but on average it contains 10g of protein, 180mg of magnesium, 80mg of calcium, 6mg of iron, 2mg of niacin per 100g. This compares well with wholemeal flour which contains 13.2g of protein, 140mg of magnesium, 35mg of calcium, 4.0mg of iron and 5.6mg of niacin per 100g.

In this recipe millet is combined with fruit purée, nuts and chopped fruit to give a pleasing texture.

100g (4 oz) millet
400–500ml (14–18 fl oz) water
50g (2 oz) flaked almonds
2 peaches weighing about 300g (11 oz), chopped
150g (5 oz) strawberries, hulled and sliced
2 medium apples weighing about 300g (11 oz)
100g (4 oz) pineapple, without skin
1 star fruit (optional decoration)

Makes 8 small servings

To give the millet a nutty taste heat it in a heavy cast-iron frying pan until it is lightly browned. Turn it over as it browns. Bring the water to the boil in a saucepan and pour in the millet. Simmer with the lid on over a low heat until the millet is soft and fluffy and all the water has been absorbed. If necessary add more water during cooking.

Mix the almonds, peaches and strawberries in a medium-sized bowl. Purée the apples and pineapple to make a sauce and stir with the millet into the chopped fruit and nuts. Chill in the fridge until ready to serve. For a special occasion garnish just before serving with thin slices of star fruit.

Each serving is 20g CHO. 120 kcals.

ICED GRAPES IN A FLAMING PINK SEA

A refreshing and easy dessert to make. Its effectiveness is in the contrast of tastes and flavours and it requires the bare minimum of preparation.

Iced grapes
225g (8 oz) seedless green
   grapes (about 48 small
   grapes)

Strawberry sauce
200g (7 oz) strawberries,
   hulled
2 tbs apple juice

Makes 4 servings

Place the grapes in a freezer bag and freeze for at least a couple of hours before you need them.

Assemble the dessert just before serving on four large dessert plates about 17.5cm (7 in) in diameter. Blend the strawberries with the apple juice in a liquidizer or food mill. Spoon the sauce over the plates. Arrange about 12 grapes on each plate. If the grapes have been in the freezer for a number of hours and are hard, leave the dessert to stand for a few minutes before serving.

Grapes assume a completely different character when frozen, astonishing the palate with sensations unmatched by any other fruit.

Each serving is 15g CHO. 50 kcals.

ORANGE FRITTERS

Oranges have long been promoted as a source of vitamin C, but marketing people seem unaware that they are also singularly rich in pectin, a type of soluble fibre. A medium-sized orange contains over 2g.

Pectin helps to reduce high blood cholesterol levels, acting like a sponge and mopping up bile salts. These are made from cholesterol, and are secreted in the small intestine after a meal to help with digestion. After they have completed their function they are partially reabsorbed. Water-soluble fibres, such as pectin, seem to engulf more of them and carry them into the large intestine where they can no longer be reabsorbed. The body then has to take cholesterol out of the blood to produce more bile salts, thus lowering the cholesterol level. Some doctors in the USA have been prescribing doses of pectin supplements to achieve these results, but you can increase your body's intake of pectin through diet; oranges and pears are both a good source. 8–10g has been shown to be enough to lower cholesterol levels – the equivalent of eating four oranges a day.

Use a heavy well-seasoned frying pan to cook the pancakes in.

Pancake batter
75g (3 oz) wholewheat flour
1 tbs wheatgerm
1 large egg
100ml (4 fl oz) skimmed milk
50–75ml (2–3 fl oz) soda
    water

Filling
2 oranges, weighing about
    375g (13 oz)

lemon or yogurt for
    decoration

Makes 4 small servings

Combine the flour and wheatgerm in a bowl. Make a well in the centre and break the egg into it. Whisk the egg with a fork and gradually add a little of the flour to make a smooth paste. Add the milk and beat in the rest of the flour. Add soda water and stand in the fridge for half an hour before using. If you leave the batter in the fridge for longer, the mixture will become thick and you will need to add an extra 25ml (1 fl oz) soda water to make a consistency suitable for coating the oranges.

Peel the oranges and remove the pith and seeds. Use a sharp knife to slice them into circles. Heat a tablespoon of oil in the frying pan. Dip each orange circle in the batter and cook in the hot oil. The batter puffs up and browns quickly. Turn over to cook on the other side. Garnish with lemon or yogurt. Serve immediately.

Each portion is 20g CHO. 125 kcals.

APPLE MERINGUE

This is a scrumptious light pudding.

500g (1lb 2 oz) eating apples,
    thinly sliced
100ml (4 fl oz) water
¼ tsp cinnamon
100g (4 oz) hazelnuts, finely
    chopped
2 egg whites
100g (4 oz) ripe banana

Makes 6 servings

Put the apples in a heavy saucepan with the water and cinnamon. Cook gently until the fruit softens and most of the water is absorbed.

Pour the hazelnuts into a 20cm (8 in) diameter pie dish. Pour in the apple and cinnamon and combine to form a soft crumbly mixture.

Whisk the egg whites into stiff peaks. Sieve the banana or put through a food mill to make it fine and liquid. Gently fold the banana into the egg whites. Pour over the apple mixture.

Bake in a preheated oven gas mark 1/ 140°C/275°F for 30 minutes or until the meringue is set and lightly browned. Serve hot.

Each portion is 15g CHO. 120 kcals.

APPLE CUSTARD

This simple quick dish is nourishing for babies and children.

450g (1 lb) eating apples
½ tsp cinnamon
150ml (5 oz) water
2 eggs

Makes 4 large servings

Slice the apples into a saucepan together with the water and cinnamon. Cook gently until the apple softens and most of the water is absorbed. Blend, using a liquidizer or food mill. Leave to cool.

Whisk the eggs and add. If you do this while the apple purée is still hot add a spoonful at a time so that the temperature of the eggs is not changed too dramatically and they become scrambled.

Pour the custard into a 20cm (8 in) diameter baking dish and bake in a preheated oven gas mark 4/180°C/350°F for 25–30 minutes until browned on top and firm. Serve immediately.

Each serving is 10g CHO. 80 kcals.

ALMOND PUDDING

This fresh fruit pudding is baked with ground nuts. It is very quick to make and useful for those who wish to exclude all flours. For a really sweet taste serve with one of the fruit sauces such as cherry or peach (see pages 155 and 156).

150g (5 oz) ground almonds
¼ tsp cinnamon
50g (2 oz) bananas, peeled and finely mashed
100g (4 oz) fresh dates with stones
100g (4 oz) fresh pineapple, without skin
2 eggs
25g (1 oz) brown rice flakes
sprinkling of cinnamon

Makes 6 servings

Combine the ground almonds, cinnamon and banana. Stone the dates and slice into thin strips. Chop the pineapple into smallish pieces and add these and the dates to the nut and banana mixture. Whisk the 2 eggs well and fold in to make a thick paste.

Pour the pudding mixture into a greased baking dish 20cm (8 in) in diameter. Mix the rice flakes with a little cinnamon in a small bowl and spoon them evenly and thinly over the top. Bake in a preheated oven gas mark 4/180°C/350°F for 30–35 minutes until browned on top. Serve hot.

Each serving is 10g CHO. 210 kcals.

NOODLE PUDDING

The Japanese wholewheat udon *noodles are very suitable for this dish and can be obtained from health food shops. These flat noodles are a creamy white colour with a delicate, light taste as the wholewheat flour used is very finely milled. Use ordinary wholewheat pasta if you cannot find these noodles.*

150g (5 oz) udon noodles

Fruit sauce
100g (4 oz) firm tofu
100g (2 oz) banana
1 medium eating apple,
   weighing about 175g
   (6 oz)
1 egg
50g (2 oz) raisins
½ tsp mixed spice
15–20g (½–¾ oz) poppy
   seeds

Makes 8 servings

Place the noodles in a saucepan of boiling water and cook until they are swollen. The way to test them is either to remove a strand and taste it or to check that the inside and outside are the same colour. Avoid overcooking. Pour them into a colander and rinse under cold water to keep the firm texture.

Prepare the sauce while the noodles are cooking: blend the tofu with the banana, apple and egg in a liquidizer or food processor. Add the raisins and mixed spice. Stir the noodles into the fruit sauce and pour into a lightly greased baking dish, 17.5–20cm (7–8 in) in diameter. Crush the poppy seeds slightly as this makes them a little stickier and sprinkle over the top.

Bake in a preheated oven gas mark 4/ 180°C/350°F for 40–50 minutes until well browned.

Each serving is 20g CHO. 125 kcals.

This dessert can be made without the raisins – each serving would then be 15g CHO. 110 kcals.

APRICOT SPONGE PUDDING

50g (2 oz) dried apricots
100ml (4 fl oz) boiling water
500g (1lb 2 oz) eating apples
100ml (4 fl oz) water
100g (4 oz) wholewheat flour
50g (2 oz) soya flour
1 tsp bicarbonate of soda
1 egg
300ml (10 fl oz) low fat
  natural yogurt
1 heaped tbs desiccated
  coconut, unsweetened

Makes 8 large servings

Soak the apricots in the boiling water for about 15 minutes.

Slice the apples into a heavy saucepan with the 100ml water. Bring to the boil then lower the heat and simmer gently for about 10 minutes until the apples have become soft, but not mushy.

Leave to cool.

Prepare the sponge mixture: blend the apricots and soaking water to a thick paste. Combine the wholewheat flour, soya flour and bicarbonate of soda in a bowl. Add the apricot paste. Whisk the egg and fold this in. Stir in the yogurt.

Grease a 20cm (8 in) diameter baking dish. Pour the cooked apples and juice evenly over the bottom of the dish. Spoon the coconut evenly over the top. Spread the sponge mixture on top of this and bake in a preheated oven gas mark 4/ 180°C/350°F for 20–30 minutes until the sponge is brown and firm on top. Serve either hot or cold.

Each serving is 20g CHO. 130 kcals.

Serving suggestion: serve with custard (see page 158).

APPLE RICE PUDDING

100g (4 oz) long grain brown rice
500ml (18 fl oz) water
225g (8 oz) eating apples, chopped
30g (1 oz, generous) prunes, stoned and chopped
½ tsp cinnamon
50g (2 oz) flaked almonds (optional) for decoration

Makes 4 servings

Place the well-washed rice in a saucepan of boiling water and let it continue to boil for about 5 minutes. Skim off any foam that rises to the surface. Add the apples, prunes and cinnamon. Turn the heat down low, put the lid on the pan and let it simmer for about 30 minutes until all the water is absorbed and the rice is soft. Brown the almonds lightly under the grill and use as a garnish. For a moister pudding serve with Orange and Strawberry Sauce (see page 155–6).

Each serving is 30g CHO. 195 kcals. Each serving with sauce is 35g CHO. 220 kcals.

APPLE CRUMBLE

Fresh or dried dates can be used in this recipe. I prefer the taste of the fresh and recommend using them when they are cheaply available in the shops. The 150g of fresh dates with stones are the carbohydrate equivalent to 50g of dried dates without stones – illustrating how much water and bulk is lost from fruit when it is dried.

This is an ideal recipe to make when first beginning to get used to sugar-free foods.

Crumble
100g (4 oz) wholewheat flour
100g (4 oz) oat bran and germ
1 tsp cinnamon
50g (2 oz) margarine or butter
1 small pear, weighing 100–125g (4–4½ oz), grated

Prepare the crumble by combining the flour, oat bran and germ and cinnamon. Rub in the fat to make thick crumbs. Stir in the pear. Put the crumble mixture to one side until it is needed.

Chop the dates and place them in the bottom of a 20cm (8 in) diameter baking dish. Pour the boiling water

Filling
50g (2 oz) dried dates or
   150g (5 oz) fresh dates
   with stones
100ml (4 fl oz) boiling water
50ml (2 fl oz) apple juice
500g (1lb 2 oz) eating apples

Makes 12 small servings

over them and crush the dates with a fork so that they become partly dissolved in the water. (There is no need to do this with fresh dates.) Add the apple juice. Slice the apples very thinly on top of the date mixture and stir them together so the apples become well coated.

Pour the crumble over the apple and dates to form an even crust. Bake in a preheated oven gas mark 4/180°C/ 350°F for 40 minutes until evenly browned on top.

Each serving is 20g CHO. 120 kcals.

STEWED FRUIT

Stewing or baking fruit is a basic part of the cooking repertoire. As all fruit contains a high proportion of water, if the fruit is cooked with a little liquid – either juice or water – this will serve to bring out the moisture in the fruit. Initially, while getting used to sugar-free fruit, you may wish to add an ounce of raisins or sultanas to give extra sweetness, but as your palate adjusts you will find that very little extra sweetener needs to be added to fresh sweet fruit.

STEWED PEARS

Surprisingly this juicy, sweet-flavoured fruit is not widely popular in Britain – we eat less per person than any other country in the EC. Yet it is a fruit that has been valued throughout history. Homer, the Greek poet, called pears 'the gift of the gods' and in Switzerland tradition had it that dreaming of ripe pears symbolized future riches and happiness.

This is a very simple method for stewing firm pears in a delicate juice. If you can find comice pears use them in this recipe.

½ eating apple, weighing just over 50g (2 oz), grated
1 tbs apple juice
250–300ml (9–10 fl oz) water
450g (1 lb) firm pears
2 large sticks cinnamon

Makes 4 servings

Put the apple in a medium-sized heavy saucepan with the apple juice and water. Bring to the boil and simmer on a low heat for 7–10 minutes until the apple has softened.

Slice the pears in half and cut out the pips. Place the pears in the pan with the insides touching the base and the skin showing outwards. Add the cinnamon sticks. Continue to simmer over a very low heat for 35–50 minutes, depending on the size of the pears. Add a little more water if the liquid seems to be disappearing.

This amount of cooking gives firm, moist stewed pears. If you prefer them softer then continue cooking, adding more water if necessary.

Remove the cinnamon sticks and serve hot or cold.

Each serving is 10g CHO. 40 kcals.

STEWED APPLE

This is a very simple way of stewing apples where the source of sweetener is the fruit themselves. Use your favourite variety of eating apple for best results. If you are in the early stages of adjusting to sugar-free food, add 25g (1 oz) raisins for a sweeter taste.

4 eating apples, weighing about 600g (1lb 5 oz), sliced
200ml (7 fl oz) water
1 tsp cinnamon

Serves 4

Put the apples in a saucepan with the water and cinnamon. Bring to the boil and simmer on a low heat until the apple has softened and absorbed the water. Serve hot or cold.

Each serving is 15g CHO. 55 kcals.

Variation: Apple Purée – blend the cooked apple. The quantity can be doubled and stored in a jug in the fridge for a couple of days.

POACHED PEACHES

The peach was cultivated in China for many centuries and eventually travelled along the caravan routes to Persia, from where the Romans took it to Italy. The leaves and flowers of the peach have traditionally been used in herbal remedies. A mixture of peach flowers was said to be good for jaundice and Culpeper, the 17th century herbalist, wrote that 'if the kernels (seeds) be bruised and boiled in vinegar, until they become thick, and applied to the head, it marvellously makes the hair to grow again upon bald places.'

4 large peaches
200ml (7 fl oz) apple juice
½ tsp cinnamon

Makes 4 servings

Cut the peaches in half. If you have difficulty removing the stones leave them in until the peaches are cooked, when they can be removed very easily.

Mix the apple juice and cinnamon together in a small heavy saucepan. Place the peaches, cut side down, into the saucepan. Simmer on a low heat for about 15 minutes until the peach flesh becomes soft but not mushy. Remove the loose skins. Serve either hot or cold with the juice.

Each serving is 15g CHO. 60 kcals.

CHERRY COMPÔTE

History has it that we should be grateful to the Romans for discovering this sweet, rich-tasting fruit in Asia Minor in about 70 BC and introducing it to Britain in the 1st century AD. During the 15th and 16th centuries the fruit stalks were used for their medicinal properties.

Dessert cherries fall into two categories: the geans which have soft flesh and the bigarreaus which have firm flesh. When buying cherries always avoid those that are split or unripe. The brief cherry season in Britain is from June to August, but it is extended by imports which begin about the middle of May. Prices start off quite high, but gradually come down as the home-grown fruit appears in the shops.

450g (1 lb) dark red cherries
200ml (7 fl oz) apple juice
2 tsp arrowroot
1 tbs kirsch (optional)

Makes 4 servings

Stone the cherries carefully, trying to keep them whole. Use either a cherry stoner or a metal skewer to push the stones through. Put the cherries and apple juice in a heavy saucepan. Bring to the boil and simmer for about 7 minutes. The length of time depends on the size of the cherries. Watch them while they are cooking because the combination of heated cherries and apple juice produces a lot of foam which can easily spill over the side of the pan.

Remove a little of the juice and combine with the arrowroot to make a smooth liquid. Return to the liquid in the pan and simmer for a further two minutes until the juice has thickened. Take off the heat. Stir in kirsch if using. Serve hot or cold.

Each serving is 20g CHO. 85 kcals.

Serving suggestion: Cherry Compôte served warm goes very well with a firm ice cream.

BAKED APPLES

The sugar-free version of this standard dessert requires minimal thought and preparation – ideal qualities for the busy cook. Use eating apples as they are not nearly as sour as cooking apples and require very little sweetening.

4 medium-sized eating apples
30g (1 oz generous) sultanas
1 tsp cinnamon
4 tbs apple juice

Makes 4 servings

Remove the cores from the apples. Place the fruit on a baking tray. Fill the centre of each apple with sultanas. Sprinkle the outside lightly with cinnamon. Spoon a tablespoon of apple juice over each apple.

Bake in a preheated oven gas mark 4/ 180°C/350°F for 30 minutes until soft.

Each apple is 20g CHO. 80 kcals.

BAKED BANANAS

The combination of banana and sesame seed makes a soft, crunchy dessert.
   A friend told me she was warned by a health visitor about giving her young child too many bananas because of their high potassium level. However, bananas contain other minerals including magnesium, small amounts of iron, copper and zinc. The potassium content in bananas is 350mg per 100g which is not a great deal more than

grapes and cantaloupe melon which are close behind with 320mg per 100g. They are also particularly high in vitamin B6 with 0.51mg per 100g compared to 0.10 in grapes or 0.07 in melons.

The misleading advice she received illustrates the risks of taking random pieces of nutritional information out of context.

400g (14 oz) bananas
4 tbs orange juice, freshly
   squeezed
100g (4 oz) sesame seeds
sprinkling of cinnamon

Makes 6 servings

Slice the bananas into slices about 0.5cm (¼ in) thick. Place in an ovenproof dish. Spoon the orange juice over the banana. Cover well with the sesame seeds. Sprinkle a little cinnamon over the bananas.

Bake in a preheated oven gas mark 4/180°C/350°F for 15 minutes until the banana has softened.

When serving, garnish the plates with any sesame seeds that have stuck to the baking dish.

Each serving is 15g CHO. 155 kcals.

9 CAKES

Cakes are the crowning glory of the tea table, the centrepiece of a well-celebrated birthday. There is a special place in one's memory for vivid images of past teas, the table adorned with the best china, an abundance of sandwiches and scones, and in the centre one glorious, mesmerizing cake.

Excluding sugar from one's life does not mean that these delights must be banished. In fact, one can enjoy cakes even more knowing that they are made healthily, that they not only look good but also actively promote well-being. Of course it is still better to eat lots of fresh or lightly cooked fruit and vegetables than lots of cake, but then cakes are special and would hold little excitement if we were to eat them every day of the week.

For me, tea with family or friends is a comfortable affair sitting around the kitchen table. Open sandwiches or rolls with do-it-yourself fillings are the norm and a cake is, of course, essential. The atmosphere is relaxed and usually rather noisy. It is very different from the At Home days that the young Constance Spry, a cookery writer, remembers at the turn of the century when visiting ladies wore white kid gloves, swishing glacé silk petticoats and immense feather boas – and children were to be seen and not heard. Preparations began first thing in the morning:

> The kitchen hummed with activity. The fire had to roar, the oven get hot, and there was to be no nonsense on the part of any one . . .
> Hanging over the banisters we children might see the feathers and hear the frou-frou and get a nice sense of party goings-on. Sometimes, indeed, unnaturally clean and restrictingly dressed, one of us might be called down 'to say how do you do'. On such occasions, until observed and called to order, I have watched

with unwavering concentration miracles of sleight of hand. I have seen tightly gloved women balance a cup and saucer in the air, negotiate a knotted veil, and convey a tremulous cucumber sandwich from hand to mouth without a fault. Seldom have I had the satisfaction of seeing even a bit of tomato misfire. The white gloves, in consideration of which the bread and butter had been rolled, might come to grief over buttery toast or too-soft sugar icing, but what of it? Such offerings on the altar of delicate behaviour only added lustre to a reputation for refinement.

Times have changed and sugar is superfluous, but the pleasures of a handsome tea are an abiding joy.

The cakes in this section are quick to make. The main work involved is the preparation of ingredients, and the actual mixing takes very little time. Food processors, blenders and electric coffee grinders can all help in speeding up the preparation process. I prefer to mix the ingredients by hand because then I know exactly what is happening to them, but the recipes will work as well if made completely by machine.

Many of the recipes are very straightforward. They combine dry ingredients with wet and have no delicate balance between the weight of sugar, eggs and flour, so it is almost impossible for them not to succeed. Bicarbonate of soda is often used as a raising agent. The only precaution to remember is to include no more liquid than specified.

The cakes stay fresh for 3 days unless the recipe specifies a shorter period. They should be wrapped with greaseproof paper and foil or stored in a tin. Their life-span is a little shorter than conventional cakes because sugar acts as a preservative. The cheesecake is best stored in the fridge.

All the cakes freeze well and should be wrapped in greaseproof paper and foil then put in a plastic freezer bag. If you intend to decorate a cake then do so after defrosting. The decoration usually looks better if freshly made.

If you are a vegan or have been told by your doctor to avoid eggs there are a number of recipes in the cake and pastry section which contain no eggs at all.

When eggs are used in a recipe beat them extremely well with a mixer or a hand whisk. They can become thick and creamy without adding sugar. After the beaten egg has been added, fold in the remaining ingredients by hand; do not use a mixer or the air incorporated in the egg will be beaten out.

APPLE CHERRY CAKE

The cherry season is so short that it is worth making a few of these cakes for cooler days and freezing them. The rich flavour of the cloves combines well with the apples and cherries. Cloves are very popular in Indonesia, not as one would expect for use in the local cuisine, but for combining with tobacco and smoking.

100g (4 oz) wholewheat flour
25g (1 oz) soya flour
100g (4 oz) ground almonds
25g (1 oz) wheatgerm
½ tsp bicarbonate of soda
1 tsp cream of tartar
½ tsp cinnamon
pinch of ground cloves
75g (3 oz) sultanas
2 large eating apples,
    weighing 300g (11 oz),
    grated
150g (5 oz) cherries, stoned
1 egg white, stiffly beaten

Makes 16 slices

Combine the flours and ground almonds, wheatgerm, bicarbonate of soda, cream of tartar and spices in a large bowl. Add the rinsed and dried sultanas to the flour mixture. Grate the apples into the bowl and stir in. Stone the cherries, cut into halves and add to the cake mixture. Bind with the stiffly beaten egg white.

Lightly grease and flour a 20cm (8 in) baking tin and pour in the cake mixture. Bake in a preheated oven gas mark 4/170°C/350°F for 30–35 minutes until a knife inserted in the centre comes out cleanly.

Each slice is 10g CHO. 90 kcals.

Serving suggestion: serve with Cherry Sauce (see page 155) or spread with Cherry Cream (see page 55).

APPLE SLICE

This moist cake uses chopped apple and a few tablespoons of apple purée as the main sweeteners. It freezes well.

½ quantity of Yeast Pastry
    (see page 92–3)

Roll out the pastry thinly to make two rectangles of about 30×20cm (12×8 in) to fit a large baking tin.

Filling
225g (8 oz) eating apples
50g (2 oz) wheatgerm
2 tsp cinnamon
700g (1lb 9 oz) eating apples, chopped
50g (2 oz) sultanas
little beaten egg for decoration

Makes 24 slices

Lightly grease the base of the tin and cover with one of the layers of pastry.

Prepare the filling: blend the 225g (8 oz) apples with a little water to make a thick purée. Combine the wheatgerm with the cinnamon and sprinkle it over the pastry base. Spread the 700g (1lb 9 oz) of chopped apples over this. Cover the apples with the sultanas and dot teaspoonsful of apple purée over the top. Put the pastry lid on and pinch the sides together. Leave to stand in a warm place for 20 minutes until the bulk has increased.

Brush with a little beaten egg and bake in a preheated oven gas mark 6/200°C/375°F for 15 minutes then turn the oven down to gas mark 5/ 190°C/375°F for a further 15–20 minutes until browned on top.

Each slice is 10g CHO. 65 kcals.

BANANA CAKE

Our local newspaper reported last year that Gwenty Cannon, prizewinner of the sugar-free cake section of the local Horticultural Society Show, had considered her own successful entry tasted revolting. I promptly challenged her to a bun-fight over tea. She fudged the Pecan Pie and minced words over my Carob Kisses, but yielded to the Poppy seed and Apple Cake and was altogether vanquished by the Banana Cake, rating it supremely light with a delicate texture. I was bowled over when she called me some days later for advice on decoration: she was making my Banana Cake for her grandson's birthday.

75g (3 oz) dried dates
100ml (4 fl oz) water
225g (8 oz) bananas, peeled
    and finely mashed
1 egg
75g (3 oz) wholewheat flour
25g (1 oz) soya flour
50g (2 oz) ground almonds
1 tsp bicarbonate of soda
½ tsp vanilla essence
150ml (5 fl oz) low-fat
    natural yogurt

Makes 16 slices

Cook the dates in the water in a
small saucepan over a low heat until
the water has been absorbed. Blend
to a smooth paste. Leave to cool.

Add the cooled date paste to the
bananas. Add the well-beaten egg.
Fold in the flour, ground almonds
and bicarbonate of soda. Stir in the
vanilla essence and yogurt.

Lightly grease and flour a 20cm
(8 in) diameter baking tin, and pour
in the mixture. Bake in a preheated
oven, gas mark 4/180°C/350°F if
your oven is a 'quick' one, but gas
mark 5/190°C/375°F if it is not
especially hot. The heat ensures that
the cake rises quickly. Bake for
35–45 minutes until the cake is
browned on top and the sides come
away from the tin.

Each slice is 10g CHO. 70 kcals.

PINEAPPLE TANG CAKE

*The fresh pineapple used in this recipe gives it a light sweet quality.
The riper the pineapple is, the sweeter the taste will be. When
testing for ripeness a good sign is if one of the fruit's inner leaves
can be pulled out easily.*

*The actual mixing of the ingredients is very quick, but preparing
them does take a little time, so it might be worth doubling the
ingredients and freezing half the cake.*

This is a useful recipe for anyone unable to eat wheat flour.

50g (2 oz) prunes, stoned and
    finely chopped
25g (1 oz) dried pear (use
    dried figs if not available)
150ml (5 fl oz) water
275g (10 oz) fresh pineapple,
    without skin

Cook the prunes, pear and water in a
saucepan over a low heat until the
water has been absorbed and the
fruit has become soft. Leave to cool.

Chop the pineapple into 1cm (½ in)
square pieces and combine with the

25g (1 oz) raisins
40g (1½ oz) pumpkin seeds
2 eggs
40g (1½ oz) ground almonds
75g (3 oz) brown rice flour

Makes 12 slices

raisins and dried fruit paste. Grind the pumpkin seeds. Whisk the eggs with a fork and add to the fruit mixture, together with the ground almonds, ground pumpkin seeds and brown rice flour. Avoid crushing the pineapple as you stir it in with the other ingredients. The mixture will be fairly thick.

Grease a 20cm (8 in) baking tin and sprinkle the surface of the tin with brown rice flour to avoid sticking. Pour in the cake mixture, smoothing the top with the back of a tablespoon. Bake in a preheated oven gas mark 4/180°C/350°F for 40 minutes until browned on top and a knife inserted in the centre comes out cleanly.

Each slice is 10g CHO. 95 kcals.

POPPY SEED AND APPLE CAKE

A thick layer of poppy seed filling and a layer of apple are packed between crisp pastry to make this unusual cake. During cooking the juice of the apples seeps down to the poppy seed filling and makes it very sweet and moist. I am not sure where the cake originates from; probably Poland or the region that used to be known as Transylvania.

I first came across this cake while studying to be a librarian. The tedium of lectures on subjects such as Bibliography of Bibliographies was broken by a visit to the warm, friendly students' cafeteria for a moan with friends and a huge slice of this cake, accompanied by a pot of yogurt. This diet sustained me through many boring lectures.

The fillings are quite time-consuming to make and all electrical aids that you possess should be enlisted to help. Failing these another pair of hands is just as good, or you could prepare the pastry in advance so that only the fillings remain to be made.

This cake improves with standing. A day after baking, the apple filling turns very jammy and is quite irresistible.

1 quantity Rough Puff Pastry
(see page 88–9)

Poppy seed filling
75g (3 oz) prunes, stoned and
finely chopped
75g (3 oz) dried dates, finely
chopped
200ml (7 fl oz) water
150g (5 oz) poppy seeds
50g (2 oz) ground almonds
200g (7 oz) firm tofu
1 egg
2 tbs orange juice
1 tbs brandy (optional)

Apple filling
500g (1lb 2 oz) eating apples
50ml (2 fl oz) apple juice

Makes 14 slices

Prepare the pastry and while it is chilling in the fridge prepare the poppy seed filling. Cook the prunes and dates in the water in a saucepan over a low heat until the water has been absorbed. The dried fruit should be quite soft and paste-like; mash it with a fork, to improve the texture.

Poppy seeds should be ground when used in a cake, to make them moister and softer. Use an electric coffee grinder, although because of its small size you will have to repeat the process a few times.

Combine the ground poppy seeds with the softened dried fruit and the ground almonds. Blend or mouli the tofu so that it becomes creamy and add. Lightly whisk the egg and fold in together with the orange juice and brandy. Put to one side.

Prepare the apple filling: thinly slice the apples and put in a saucepan with the apple juice. Simmer over a low heat with the lid on for about 10 minutes until the apples are softened. Remove from the heat and leave to cool while rolling out the pastry.

Divide the pastry into two halves, one slightly larger than the other. Roll out the larger one to a 28×23cm (11×9 in) rectangle. Take a baking dish which is about 25.5×20cm (10×8 in) and line with the pastry. There will be extra pastry to cover the sides of the baking dish. Roll out the smaller piece of pastry to make a lid.

To assemble: spread the poppy seed filling evenly over the base of the pastry. Pour the apples and their juice over the top of the poppy seed filling. Put the pastry lid on top and pinch the pastry together at the sides.

Bake in a preheated oven gas mark 5/ 170°C/350°F for about 40–45 minutes until the pastry is browned.

Each slice is 20g CHO. 190 kcals.

CAROB CAKE

75g (3 oz) raisins
100ml (4 fl oz) water
125g (4½ oz) wholewheat flour
15g (½ oz) wheatgerm
30g (generous 1 oz) low fat soya flour
50g (2 oz) carob powder
1 tsp bicarbonate of soda
2 tsp cream of tartar
50ml (2 fl oz) oil
200g (7 oz) pear, grated
2 eggs
100ml (4 fl oz) low-fat natural yogurt

Makes 10 large slices

Cook the raisins and water in a saucepan over a low heat until all the water has been absorbed. Blend to make into a paste. Leave to cool.

In a large bowl mix together the wholewheat flour, wheatgerm and soya flour, carob powder, bicarbonate of soda and cream of tartar. Stir in the oil. Add the raisin paste and grated pear. Whisk the eggs well until creamy and add to the cake mixture. Add the yogurt to make a mixture with a thick pouring consistency.

Pour into a greased and floured 20cm (8 in) diameter baking tin and bake in a preheated oven gas mark 4/ 180°C/350°F for 30–35 minutes until a knife inserted in the centre comes out cleanly.

Each slice is 20g CHO. 155 kcals.

Variation: cover with Carob Icing (see page 56) and sprinkle 1 tbs of desiccated coconut over the top.

CAROB MOUSSE LAYER CAKE

This impressive multi-layered cake has four layers of carob mousse set between four layers of sponge. It is a small rectangular shape about 12.5cm (5 in) high.

75g (3 oz) dried dates
100ml (4 fl oz) water
150g (5 oz) wholewheat flour
25g (1 oz) soya flour
25g (1 oz) wheatgerm
1 tsp bicarbonate of soda
2 tsp cream of tartar
½ tsp vanilla essence
50g (2 oz) banana, peeled
   and mashed
2 eggs, size 3
300ml (10 fl oz) low fat
   natural yogurt

½ quantity of Carob Mousse
   (see page 000)

Makes 20 slices

Cook the dates and water in a small saucepan over a low heat until all the water has been absorbed. Blend to make a smooth paste. Leave to cool.

Combine the flour, wheatgerm, bicarbonate of soda and cream of tartar. Add the cooled dates, vanilla essence, mashed banana and well-beaten eggs. Fold in the yogurt to make a creamy mixture.

Grease and flour a swiss roll tin about 30×23cm (12×9 in) square. Spoon the cake mixture evenly over the tin. Bake in a preheated oven gas mark 4/180°C/350°F for about 30 minutes until the cake has browned and is firm. Remove carefully with a palate knife and leave to cool.

Prepare the Carob Mousse.

Cut the cake in quarters, so that each piece is about 15×11cm (6×4½ in). Spread the Carob Mousse over each layer of cake, and place the layers one on top of another, with a layer of Carob Mousse on top. Ensure that the top layer is slightly thicker than the others because if it is too thin it will dry out and spoil the effect. Some of the filling will ooze out because of the weight of the layers, but simply spread this around the sides.

Each slice is 10g CHO. 75 kcals.

CARROT CAKE

This light Carrot Cake is perfumed with orange peel, giving off a fragrant orange scent while it bakes. The smell always reminds me of cold winters spent working in a library in Jerusalem. The old stone building was wonderfully cool in the long hot summer, but bitterly cold in the winter months. We used two regulation pot-bellied open paraffin stoves to heat the library, which were quite effective although they gave off suffocating fumes. The window should have been opened to allow the fumes to escape, but that would have allowed the cold to come back in. We found our way round this problem by eating seasonal oranges and balancing the peel precariously on the metal bars covering the flames. After a few moments the heat would draw out the orange perfume from the skin and we were intoxicated by the powerful odour.

100g (4 oz) dried dates, chopped
100ml (4 fl oz) water
225g (8 oz) carrots, grated finely
75g (3 oz) wholewheat flour
25g (1 oz) wheatgerm
25g (1 oz) desiccated coconut
50g (2 oz) ground almonds
1 tsp bicarbonate of soda
½–1 tsp mixed spice
1 egg
1 tsp grated orange zest
150ml (5 fl oz) low fat natural yogurt

Makes 12 slices

Cook the dates and water in a small saucepan over a low heat until the water has been absorbed. Mash with a fork to make a smooth paste, and blend if necessary. Put them to one side to cool. Grate the carrots and mix with the cooled date paste.

Combine the flour, wheatgerm, coconut, ground almonds, bicarbonate of soda and spice. Stir in the carrots and dates. Add the well-beaten egg and the orange zest. Fold in the yogurt.

Pour into a greased and floured 20cm (8 in) diameter baking tin. Bake in a preheated oven gas mark 5/190°C/375°F for 40 minutes until the cake has browned on top and the sides have begun to come away from the tin.

Each slice is 10g CHO. 100 kcals.

PARSNIP CAKE

This is a very fragrant light cake although a parsnip may sound an unlikely candidate for providing such qualities!

Parsnip contains, per 100g, 1mg of vitamin E, 10mg of vitamin C, very small amounts of the B vitamins and a number of minerals, including potassium, phosphorus and magnesium. Parsnip, and particularly wild parsnip, was used for medicinal purposes. The root was chopped into a pulp and used as a poultice to relieve and heal abscesses and swellings, while the juice was claimed by Culpeper, the 17th century physician and astrologer, to cure jaundice.

225g (8 oz) parsnips
75g (3 oz) wholewheat flour
50g (2 oz) soya flour
50g (2 oz) ground almonds
1 tsp bicarbonate of soda
2 tsp cream of tartar
1 tsp cinnamon
75g (3 oz) dried dates, chopped
50g (2 oz) prunes, stoned and chopped
100ml (4 fl oz) water
6 tbs orange juice, freshly squeezed
1 heaped tsp of orange zest
1 egg
150ml (5 fl oz) low fat natural yogurt

Makes 8 large slices

Scrub the parsnip well then grate.

Combine the flours, ground almonds, bicarbonate of soda, cream of tartar and cinnamon. Stir in the grated parsnip.

Cook the chopped dates, prunes and water in a small saucepan over a low heat until the water has been absorbed. If necessary blend to make a smooth paste.

Add the date–prune paste, orange juice and zest to the flours. Whisk the egg well and add. Stir in the yogurt.

Pour into a greased and floured 20cm (8 in) diameter baking tin and bake in a preheated oven gas mark 5/ 190°C/375°F for 30–40 minutes until firm.

Each slice is 20g CHO. 160 kcals.

CHERRY CHEESECAKE

This is a delicious cheesecake. The cherries make it very sweet and special.

Crust
10g (½ oz) carob powder
6 tbs water
15g (½ oz) sultanas, chopped
(use dried dates if not available)
50g (2 oz) shredded wheat

Filling
2 eggs
150g (5 oz) bananas, peeled
200ml (7 oz) skimmed milk quark
75g (3 oz) low fat natural yogurt
25g (1 oz) ground almonds
a few drops of vanilla essence
100g (4 oz) cherries

Topping
½ tsp agar-agar
100ml (4 fl oz) apple juice
200g (7 oz) cherries

Makes 12 slices

Prepare the base: put the carob powder, water and chopped sultanas in a small saucepan. Place over a low heat stirring all the time. The carob powder will dissolve in the liquid and the sultanas will become mushy. Take the pan off the heat and add the shredded wheat, crumbling it in with your fingers. Stir until all the shredded wheat is coated with the carob sauce. Press into a 20cm (8 in) diameter greased baking tin, patting the soft mixture with your fingertips so that it is distributed over the whole tin.

Prepare the filling: whisk the eggs well. Mouli or sieve the bananas to a fine liquid and add to the eggs. Whisk for a further minute. Fold in the quark and yogurt. Add the ground almonds and vanilla essence. Add the 100g (4 oz) of cherries, stoned and halved. Stir carefully so that they do not become mashed or the cake mixture turns pink. This is the reason that they are added at the end.

Spoon the filling over the base and bake in a preheated oven gas mark 4/180°C/350°F for 25–30 minutes until the mixture becomes firm and slightly browned at the edges. Cheesecake continues to set even when taken out of the oven so do not overcook.

Prepare the topping: combine the agar-agar with a dessertspoon of the apple juice, then add the remainder. Bring to the boil in a very small pan and allow it to bubble gently for one minute. Pour the jelly over the surface of the cold cake. Quickly arrange the 200g (7 oz) of stoned and halved cherries on top of the cheesecake. They will set firmly in the jelly.

Each slice is 10g CHO. 70 kcals.

YEAST CHEESECAKE

Use fromage frais with just under 4 per cent fat for this recipe. If you cannot obtain it from your local grocers or supermarket substitute skimmed milk quark.

For a really sweet taste spread 25g (1 oz) of sugar-free apricot jam over the pastry base.

½ quantity Yeast Pastry (see page 92)

Filling
100g (4 oz) cottage cheese
400g (14 oz) low-fat fromage frais
150g (5 oz) raisins
2 tsp lemon zest
1 egg
little beaten egg for decoration

Makes 24 slices

Roll out the pastry thinly to make two equal-sized rectangles to fit a 25×20cm (10×8 in) baking tin. Lightly grease the base of the tin and cover it with one of the pastry sheets.

Put the cottage cheese through a food mill so that it becomes fine and combine with the fromage frais. Add the raisins, lemon zest and well-beaten egg.

Spread the cheese mixture over the base of the pastry. Place the lid on top. Leave to stand in a warm room for 20 minutes until it has increased in size. Brush the lid with a little beaten egg and make a few slashes across the top of the pastry.

Bake in a preheated oven gas mark 6/ 200°C/400°F for 15 minutes then turn the oven down to gas mark 5/ 190°C/375°F and cook for a further 15 minutes until browned.

Each slice is 10g CHO. 75 kcals.

PERSIMMON CHEESECAKE

Persimmons, round, smooth, orange-skinned fruit, have a unique taste if they are eaten when just ripe. The kaki variety was originally found growing in Japan and China, and is sometimes known as a Chinese apple, probably because of its origins. The Israelis grow sharon fruit which are smaller versions of persimmons and can be substituted for them in this recipe.

The persimmon is a nutritious fruit. Each one contains about 500mcg of carotene (vitamin A) and 10mg of vitamin C. This compares well with an apple which contains only 30mcg of carotene and 3mg of vitamin C.

This recipe has a very delicate taste as it is sweetened solely with the ripe fruit. The persimmon is ready for use when it is a little soft to the touch and may even have a slight tinge of brown in the orange skin. If it is eaten when unripe and still hard it has an unpleasant astringent taste. The Chinese extract a fluid from it when it is in this state and use it to make cosmetics.

The filling is not baked but set with agar-agar.

1 quantity of Sweet Seed
  Pastry (see page 91–2)

Filling
600g (1 lb 4 oz) ripe
  persimmon, peeled
200g (7 oz) skimmed milk
  quark
100g (4 oz) Greek yogurt
1 egg, separated
2 heaped tbs agar-agar flakes
100ml (4 fl oz) apple juice,
  unsweetened
50ml (2 fl oz) water

Makes 12 slices

Lightly grease a 23cm (9 in) diameter baking tin or deep baking dish, and pat the pastry around the base. Bake in a preheated oven gas mark 4/ 180°C/350°F for 20–25 minutes until the pastry is cooked and lightly browned all over.

Prepare the filling: blend the persimmon to make about 350ml (12 fl oz) of fruit purée. Combine with the quark, yogurt and well-beaten egg yolk.

Mix the agar-agar flakes with the

apple juice, water and about 100ml (4 fl oz) of the fruit purée in a small saucepan. Bring to the boil and simmer for at least 5 minutes, stirring all the time. Add to the fruit and cheese mixture, stirring the setting liquid in well. Whisk the egg white and fold in. Pour over the cooked pastry base and leave to set. Chill in the fridge before serving.

Each slice is 15g CHO. 130 kcals.

TOFU APPLE CHEESECAKE

Tofu is a very effective non-milk substitute for curd cheese. The main difference in texture is that tofu is firmer.

1 quantity Sweet Seed Pastry (see page 91–2)

Filling
500g (1lb 2 oz) eating apples, chopped
100ml (4 fl oz) water
200g (7 oz) firm tofu
1 egg
2 tbs lemon juice, freshly squeezed
1 tsp cinnamon
1 tsp vanilla essence
30g (1 oz generous) ground almonds
25g (1 oz) brown rice flakes

Makes 12 large slices

Prepare the pastry. Take a 23cm (9 in) baking tin. Pat the dough around the base of the tin. Bake blind in a preheated oven gas mark 4/180°C/ 350°F for 10 minutes.

Prepare the filling: combine the apple with the water and blend in a liquidizer to make a purée. Add the tofu and continue to blend until a thick paste is formed. Fold in the whisked egg, lemon juice, cinnamon, vanilla essence and ground almonds.

Pour the filling into the partly baked crust. Sprinkle the top with the brown rice flakes. Return to the oven at gas mark 4/180°C/350°F for 30 minutes until browned around the edges.

Each slice is 10g CHO. 115 kcals.

Sponges and Light Cakes

SWISS ROLL

Traditional recipes for Swiss Roll are always precise, with the weight of the dry ingredients often balanced against the weight of the eggs. Swiss Roll is basically a light, flexible sponge and it presents particular problems for the sugar-free cook. It is not possible to use much dried fruit, even if it is blended, because it will affect the lightness of the sponge and the degree of ease with which it can be rolled up without cracking at each turn. To overcome the problem this recipe uses sieved banana for sweetness.

The texture of the Swiss Roll is also improved by the amount of air beaten in with the eggs. Although the sponge is simple to make it is sensitive, so it is important to avoid delays when mixing and baking. When you take the Swiss Roll out of the oven have everything you need ready at hand so that you can roll it up quickly while it is still warm.

Spread with a sugar-free jam or for special occasions fill with Creme aux Marrons (see page 170–1).

125g (4½ oz) bananas, peeled
50g (2 oz) fine milled wholewheat flour
25g (1 oz) dried dates
100ml (4 fl oz) water
3 eggs
25g (1 oz) ground almonds
½ tsp almond essence
2 tbs desiccated coconut, unsweetened
50g (2 oz) sugar-free jam

Makes 12 thin slices

Grease or oil the base of a 23×30cm (9×12 in) swiss roll tin and place a sheet of grease-proof paper on top. Oil the top surface of the grease-proof paper so that it fits snugly into the corners and sides of the tin. Preheat the oven to gas mark 6/ 200°C/400°F.

Prepare the ingredients: put the banana through a food mill or sieve it into a small bowl. Heat the dates in a pan with water until all the water is absorbed, and mark finely with a fork. Sieve the flour, after which there will be a small residue of coarse grains at the bottom of the sieve. Try and force them through. Toss back whatever remains into the sieved flour.

Separate the yolks and whites of the eggs into two bowls. Whisk the egg yolks until pale and creamy. Add the liquid banana and continue to whisk for a little longer. Whisk in date paste. Whisk the egg whites stiffly and fold these into the banana and egg yolk mixture. Add the sieved flour, ground almonds and almond essence and stir in gently with a metal spoon.

Pour into the prepared swiss roll tin and spread evenly making sure you do not skimp near the corners. Bake for 7–10 minutes in the centre of the oven until the mixture has set and is beginning to brown. If it becomes too brown or overcooked it will crack when rolled up.

Have ready prepared a sheet of greaseproof paper the same size as the baking tin and placed on top of a clean tea towel. Sprinkle the greaseproof sheet with desiccated coconut.

Take the Swiss Roll out of the oven and turn it top side down on to the coconut-covered paper. Using a sharp knife gently ease the greaseproof lining paper off the back of the Swiss Roll. The corners and the sides are often the most brittle spots so approach these first. While the Swiss Roll is still warm swiftly roll it up in the greaseproof paper and tea towel. When cool ease open, lightly spread the jam over the surface and roll up again.

Each slice is 5g CHO. 70 kcals.

CAROB SWISS ROLL

This recipe shatters the usual image of heavy wholefood cakes. Fill it with Hazelnut–Carob Cream (see page 55) and it can shoulder its way on to a tea table with the best.

It can also be used as a basis for a Yuletide log. Fill with fromage frais mixed with seasonal fruit such as sliced bananas or chopped clementines and decorate the outside with half the recipe for Carob Mousse (see page 164).

3 eggs
125g (4½ oz) bananas, peeled
25g (1 oz) dried dates
100ml (4 fl oz) water
50g (2 oz) wholewheat flour, finely milled
25g (1 oz) carob powder
few drops of vanilla essence
2 tbs desiccated coconut, unsweetened
50g (2 oz) sugar-free jam

Makes 12 slices

This recipe is prepared in the same way as Swiss Roll. The basic outline for preparing this cake is given below, but the Swiss Roll recipe (see pages 147–8) provides a more detailed explanation.

Prepare a swiss roll tin by greasing the base, covering it with greaseproof paper then greasing the top of the paper. Preheat the oven to gas mark 6/200°C/400°F.

Separate the eggs. Whisk the egg yolks until pale and creamy. Add the sieved or moulied banana and whisk a little longer. Whisk the egg whites stiffly and fold in. Add the sieved flour, carob powder and vanilla essence. Fold in with a metal spoon.

Pour into the prepared swiss roll tin and spread evenly making sure you do not skimp near the corners. Bake for 7–10 minutes in the centre of the oven until the mixture has set. If it is overcooked it will crack when rolled up.

Remove from the oven and turn on to a sheet of greaseproof paper resting on a tea towel. The greaseproof paper should be sprinkled with desiccated coconut. Using a sharp knife gently ease the greaseproof lining paper off the back of the Swiss Roll. Swiftly roll up the Swiss Roll in the greaseproof lining paper and tea towel while it is still warm. When cool ease open, lightly spread the filling over the surface and roll up again.

Each slice without filling is 5g CHO. 65 kcals.

APRICOT FAIRY CAKES

These little sponge cakes are very light. Cook in paper cases, decorate with Coconut Icing and a little blob of apricot jam in the middle and they look and taste quite mouthwatering.

50g (2 oz) dried apricots
3 eggs, separated
125g (4½ oz) bananas
25g (1 oz) dried dates
100ml (4 fl oz) water
25g (1 oz) ground almonds
50g (2 oz) wholewheat flour, finely milled
1 quantity Coconut Icing (see page 00)
1 dessertspoon strawberry jam

Makes 15 cakes

Pour a little boiling water over the dried apricots and leave to stand for half an hour. Put the apricots and soaking water in a small saucepan and heat until the water has been absorbed. Chop the apricots finely. Heat the dates and water in a pan until the water is absorbed, and mark finely with a fork.

Whisk the egg yolks until they are thick and creamy. Whisk in the moulied banana (Sieve if you do not have a mouli – the aim is to remove all lumps.) Whisk in the date paste. Whisk the egg whites until stiff and fold in. Fold in the ground almonds, sieved flour and chopped apricots with a metal spoon. Spoon the mixture into 15 paper cases.

Bake in a preheated oven gas mark 5/
190°C/375°F for 8–10 minutes. The
little cakes will puff up and turn
brown on top in that short space of
time, although they drop slightly
after being taken out of the oven.

*2 cakes with Coconut Icing are 10g
CHO. 115 kcals.*

POPPY SEED TORTE

*Poppy seeds are often used in cakes in Eastern Europe, but in
Britain are mostly used for decorating bread or rolls. The blue-
black seeds are high in thiamin, one of the B vitamins. Herbalists
recommend them as a general tonic food and in parts of Turkey
they are mixed into a health-boosting cake.*

50ml (2 fl oz) boiling water
75g (3 oz) dried dates,
  chopped
25g (1 oz) prunes, stoned and
  chopped
175g (6 oz) poppy seeds
175g (6 oz) ground almonds
50g (2 oz) soya flour
500g (1lb 2 oz) ripe pears,
  grated
1 tbs brandy (optional)
4 eggs, separated

Makes 12 slices

Pour the boiling water over the dates
and prunes. Leave to stand for 15
minutes then purée in a blender.
Alternatively increase the quantity of
water to 150ml (5 fl oz), chop the
dried fruit finely and put them in a
small saucepan to simmer over a low
heat until the water is absorbed and
the dried fruit has become a thick
paste.

Grind the poppy seeds in an electric
coffee grinder. Combine them with
the ground almonds and soya flour.
Add the pear to the dry ingredients
together with the dried fruit purée,
brandy and beaten egg yolks. Whisk
the egg whites until stiff and fold
into the mixture.

Grease and flour two 20–23cm
(8–9 in) diameter sandwich tins.
Divide the mixture equally between
them and bake in a preheated oven
gas mark 4/180°C/350°F for about

25–30 minutes until the cakes are brown on top and a knife inserted in the middle comes out easily. Leave to cool befor removing from the tins.

When cool the cake can be filled with fromage frais mixed with sieved banana or Apricot–Almond Spread (see page 53).

Each slice without filling is 10g CHO. 235 kcals.

WALNUT CAKE

This moist cake can be eaten by itself or served with a fruity cream such as Clementine Cream Delight (see page 112–13).

Walnuts are a high source of Omega 3 fatty acids. These are mostly found in fish oils and come from very few plant sources. The beneficial effects of these oils include lowering of blood cholesterol levels and reducing certain types of arthritic pain. A survey of heart disease mortality in Holland showed a 50 per cent lower death rate from heart disease amongst men eating at least one fish meal a week compared to those who eat none. Walnuts contain 1.9g Omega 3 per 100g, not as high as mackerel which contains 2.6g, but rather higher than soya beans which contain 0.85g.

50g (2 oz) dried dates, finely chopped
200g (7 oz) walnuts, ground
50g (2 oz) soya flour
25g (1 oz) wheatgerm
¼–½ tsp cinnamon
1 tsp bicarbonate of soda
2 tsp cream of tartar
150g (5 oz) bananas, peeled and finely mashed
3 eggs

Makes 10 large slices

Cover the dates with a little water and leave to soak for 20 minutes.

Combine the ground walnuts, soya flour, wheatgerm, cinnamon, bicarbonate of soda and cream of tartar. Mix the banana with the soaked dates. Separate the eggs and whisk the egg yolks until they are thick and creamy and add to the nut mixture. Whisk the egg whites stiffly and fold into the mixture. Grease and flour a 20cm (8 in) square baking tin and pour in the mixture. Bake in a

preheated oven gas mark 4/180°C/
350°F for 25 minutes until evenly
browned.

Each slice is 10g CHO. 180 kcals.

FRUIT CAKE

*Fruit cake is often the basis for a festive cake for a wedding or
anniversary or for a Christmas tea. Everyone has their favourite
combinations of dried fruit. This recipe uses the traditional raisins
and dates, but also includes dried apricots and dried bananas.
Dried bananas are sticky and sweet and contain 2mg of vitamin
B6 per 100g.*

*Baking a fruit cake can be a long slow process and I have come
across various tips to avoid it drying out. Some people swear by
putting a baking dish of hot water in the oven which adds
moisture to the cooking environment, while others cover the top
with greaseproof paper throughout cooking. If you are not keen on
a hard crust then a sheet of greaseproof paper cut to size and put
on the top of the cake after the first 50–60 minutes is a useful
protection. Another method is not to make the fruit cake too deep
so that it does not require such extensive baking.*

*The attraction of a fruit cake is that it can be prepared in
advance for a special occasion. This still holds true for a sugar-free
version, but it keeps for less time. A method for encouraging its
preserving qualities is to pour fruit juice or spirits such as brandy
slowly over the top of the finished cake so that it soaks through.
Wrap well with greaseproof paper and foil and leave to mature in a
tin for a couple of weeks.*

100g (4 oz) dried figs
75g (3 oz) dried apricots
75g (3 oz) dried bananas
100g (4 oz) dried dates
100g (4 oz) seedless raisins
100g (4 oz) sultanas
100ml (4 fl oz) water
100g (4 oz) firm tofu
50g (2 oz) butter
1 tbs tahini
2 large eggs

Soak all the dried fruit except the
dates in the water for 30 minutes.
After soaking, rinse, dry and chop
the dried figs, apricots and bananas.
Put the dates with a little water in a
separate bowl.

If you are using a food processor
combine the dates with the tofu,
butter, tahini and eggs to make a
sweet batter. Alternatively chop the

50g (2 oz) whole almonds,
    with outer skins, chopped
50g (2 oz) ground almonds
100g (4 oz) wholewheat flour
25g (1 oz) soya flour
1 tsp bicarbonate of soda
2 tsp cream of tartar
1 tsp mixed spice
1 tsp lemon zest
1 large orange weighing
    about 175g (6 oz) or
    100ml (4 fl oz) orange
    juice
brandy (optional)

Makes 16 slices

dates very finely and mash as much as you can with the back of a fork and add to the well-whisked eggs, moulied tofu, creamed butter and tahini. Pour this mixture over the dried fruit together with the chopped almonds. Stir well and add all the remaining ingredients except for the orange. This should make a very stiff cake mixture.

Pour into a 20cm (8 in) diameter cake tin which has been oiled and lined with oiled greaseproof paper. Flatten the top with the back of a spoon.

Bake in a preheated oven gas mark 3/170°C/325°F for 60 minutes until the top is well browned and a knife inserted in the centre comes out cleanly.

When the cake has cooled, squeeze the juice from the orange, which should make about 100ml (4 fl oz). Make a few light cuts on the top of the cake and slowly pour the juice over until it has all soaked in. If you prefer your fruit cake more alcoholic then substitute a little brandy for the orange juice. Wrap the cake in greaseproof paper and foil and store in a tin for one week to mature before using.

Each slice is 25g CHO. 185 kcals.

10 SAUCES

CHERRY SAUCE

This sauce requires no cooking. Try and use the dark red cherries as these have the sweetest flavour. Cherries are high in potassium and contain magnesium, a small amount of calcium and some of the B vitamins.

150g (5 oz) cherries, stoned
1 tbs apple juice

Makes 150ml (5 fl oz)

Blend the cherries with the apple juice to make a thick liquid. Serve immediately or chill until needed later the same day.

Sauce is 15g CHO. 70 kcals.

Serving suggestion: serve with Apple Cherry Cake (see page 134).

ORANGE AND STRAWBERRY SAUCE

This is a thick jam-like sauce. Use English strawberries because they are the sweetest.

1 large orange, weighing
    about 200g (7 oz)
100g (4 oz) strawberries,
    hulled
1 scant tsp arrowroot
1 dessertspoon brandy

Makes 4 servings

Peel the orange and remove all the pith and any pips. Blend the orange and strawberries in a liquidizer. The purée will be a salmon colour. Pour it into a small saucepan, removing a small amount to mix with the arrowroot. Pour this into the pan with the rest of the purée. Heat on a low light until the purée thickens. Serve either hot or cold.

Sauce is 20g CHO. 100 kcals.

Serving suggestions: this sauce goes well with ice cream. It can also be used to make a speedy dessert – serve the sauce with firm fresh fruit such as apricots, sliced bananas or quartered pears.

PASTEL PINK SAUCE

350g (12 oz) strawberries, hulled
1 eating apple, weighing about 125g (4½ oz)
1 tbs apple juice

Blend the strawberries, apple and apple juice in a liquidizer and chill in the fridge until needed. Use the same day.

Sauce is 35g CHO. 140 kcals.

Serving suggestion: serve with Chilled Almond Globes (see page 000).

PEACH SAUCE

'An apple is an excellent thing – until you have tried a peach!'
George du Maurier, 19th-century French–English artist and novelist.

There is something special about peaches, whether it is the texture, colour or smell of the fruit, or a combination of all three. When buying peaches make sure they are firm and a rich warm colour – a sign that they are ready for eating.

3 peaches, weighing about 375g (13 oz)
2 tbs apple juice
⅛ tsp ground ginger
1 dessertspoon brandy

Wash two of the peaches and slice into the liquidizer. Blend with the apple juice and ground ginger to make 300ml (½ pt) liquid.

Pour boiling water over the remaining peach. Remove the skin, cut the fruit into thin slices and add to the sauce.

Heat in a small saucepan and bring to the boil. Take off the heat and stir in the brandy.

Sauce is 35g CHO. 160 kcals.

Serving suggestion: serve with Peach Ice Cream (see page 176) or Apple Crumble (see page 125–6).

RASPBERRY SAUCE

The raspberries sold in the shops are all cultivated, but if you live near woods where raspberries grow wild it is worth searching them out. Herbalists regard wild raspberries and their leaves as having considerable medicinal powers. Raspberry leaf tea is a well known tonic taken during pregnancy and sometimes during labour.

Cultivated raspberries also have a high mineral and vitamin content – 220mg of potassium, 41mg of calcium, 22mg of magnesium, 1.2mg of iron, 17mg of selenium, 25mg of vitamin C, some carotene and some of the B-complex vitamins. They are also low in calories.

1 small eating apple, weighing about 100g (4 oz)
75ml (3 fl oz) apple juice, unsweetened
275g (10 oz) raspberries

Slice the apple into a medium-sized saucepan with the apple juice. Bring to the boil and simmer until the apple has softened. Add the raspberries and mash slightly with a fork. Bring to the boil and remove from the heat. Sieve the sauce and serve cold.

The sauce is 35g CHO. 140 kcals.

Serving suggestions: serve with Melon and Raspberry Ice Cream (see page 174). If you double the quantity Raspberry Sauce can be served by itself in little bowls.

CUSTARD

It was a particularly difficult task to work out how to sweeten custard subtly without affecting its pure yellow colour and texture. I turned to Judy Jackson, a cookery writer and demonstrator, who had the original idea of infusing the sweet flavour of dried apricots into the custard – without using the fruit itself.

50g (2 oz) dried apricots
75ml (3 fl oz) boiling water
2 large egg yolks
1 tsp arrowroot
150–175ml (5–6 fl oz)
    skimmed milk

Pour the boiling water over the apricots and leave to stand for an hour.

Lightly beat the egg yolks with a fork then add the arrowroot. Carefully pour the water off the dried apricots into a measuring jug (keep the dried apricots as they will be used for further infusion) and add enough of the milk to make the liquid up to 225ml (8 fl oz).

Heat the milk and apricot water in a small saucepan to just below boiling point. Pour over the yolks and arrowroot, stirring. Pour the mixture back into the pan and cook on a very low heat stirring continuously with a wooden spoon until it thickens and coats the back of the spoon. The slow thickening is very important. If the contents of the pan seem to be getting too hot and it is not possible to lower the cooking heat any more, lift the saucepan a little way above the heat for a couple of seconds to slow down the cooking. Another alternative is to use a double saucepan, but this is not essential. The custard should not be allowed to boil as this causes curdling.

When the custard has thickened pour it over the apricots and leave for 20–30 minutes. Sieve before using.

Custard is 15g CHO. 180 kcals.

BANANA CUSTARD

This custard goes very well with crumbles and pies and requires less preparation than the plain custard recipe.

2 large egg yolks
1 tsp arrowroot
225ml (8 fl oz) skimmed milk
50g (2 oz) ripe banana,
    peeled

Lightly beat the egg yolks with a fork then add the arrowroot.

Heat the milk in a small saucepan to just below boiling point. Pour over the yolks, stirring. Pour the egg and milk mixture back into the pan and cook on a very low heat. Stir continuously with a wooden spoon until the mixture thickens and coats the back of the spoon. The slow thickening is very important. If the contents of the pan seem to be getting too hot, lift it a little way above the heat for a couple of seconds to slow down the cooking. The custard should not be allowed to boil as this causes curdling. (If that does happen some cooks recommend pouring the mixture immediately into a bowl and whisking it in order to get back to a fairly smooth texture.)

When the custard has thickened pour it into a bowl and add the finely mashed banana. Sieve the custard and either use hot or leave to cool.

Banana custard is 25g CHO. 240 kcals.

11 MOUSSES, JELLIES, CREAMS AND ICE CREAMS

Agar-Agar

Agar-agar is a seaweed and a very effective setting agent for mousses and jellies; it comes in either powder form or flakes. Powder is the form most readily available in health food chains, while specialist health food shops will stock the flakes. Both are soluble in hot water but not in cold. They set quickly and do not need to be refrigerated to speed up the gelling process.

Agar-agar flakes are prepared by slow cooking, filtering and, according to the manufacturers, being placed out 'in the winter snow to be naturally bleached and freeze dried into dry fibrous strips'. These are then cut into flakes. The quantity of flakes used is normally double that of powder.

I find the flakes work best with mousses while the powder, which requires a shorter cooking time, is more suitable for jellies. The flakes set more slowly which can be useful when other ingredients have to be added after the agar-agar.

How to use agar-agar flakes: mix the flakes with the liquid in a small pan. Slowly bring to the boil and simmer for 5 minutes, stirring all the time. Use a very small pan if the quantity of liquid is below 200ml (7 fl oz) so that less water evaporates during the simmering. If the liquid seems to be evaporating too fast, quickly add a little more to the pan.

How to use agar-agar powder: dissolve the powder in a little liquid to make a thick paste then gradually add the rest of the liquid. Bring to the boil in a pan, the size depending on the amount of liquid, and boil for 1½ minutes. This sets very quickly. If only using a little liquid with the powder, be careful that it does not evaporate too fast or you will be left with a glutinous mass instead of liquid in the pan.

Ice Cream

Home-made ice cream is delicious. If you use an ice cream machine this makes a great difference to the texture because the mixture is kept in continuous motion throughout the freezing time which results in a smooth, light texture. The alternative method is to remove the ice cream from the freezer after about an hour, beat it to break up the ice crystals, and return it again to the freezer. This can be repeated a few times, although the result will be icier than ice cream made with a machine. I find that if there is a lot of fruit in the ice cream this compensates for the firmer texture. A third method, which also originates from the USA, is to freeze the fruit first then mix with yogurt or cream in a food processor.

When the ice cream is made, avoid thawing and refreezing as this will make its texture coarser. Ideally make as much as you need at one go or else divide the quantity into two freezer containers.

STRAWBERRY MOUSSE

Strawberries 'cool the liver, the blood and the spleen, or a hot choleric stomach; refresh and comfort fainting spirits and quench thirst', wrote Culpeper in the 17th century. A modern-day herbalist, Juliette de Bairacli Levy, claims that strawberries act as a nerve tonic and are good for treating anaemia, lowered vitality and lack of appetite. Interestingly she suggests that 'strawberry rash' is not an allergic reaction, but evidence of the cleansing action of strawberries, driving excess acid from the body more speedily than the body can remove it by other means. Wild strawberries are richer in iron, but any kind make this marvellous mousse.

300g (11 oz) strawberries, hulled
150g (5 oz) Greek yogurt
100ml (4 fl oz) water
100ml (4 fl oz) apple juice
1 tbs agar-agar flakes
150g (5 oz) strawberries, hulled and sliced

Makes 4 small servings

Blend the 300g (11 oz) strawberries to make a purée. Combine with the yogurt.

Put the water, apple juice and agar-agar flakes in a small saucepan. Bring to the boil and stir for 5 minutes while it simmers. Keep on stirring to avoid the agar-agar sticking to the sides of the pan. Take off the heat and add to the strawberry and yogurt mixture. Add the 150g (5 oz) sliced strawberries. Spoon into 4 glasses or bowls and leave to set.

Each serving is 10g CHO. 90 kcals.

PINEAPPLE AND APPLE MOUSSE

This is a delicate, fluffy dessert. Make sure the pineapple you use is ready for eating. An unripe one will not only sour the dessert, but can act as a stomach irritant for some people. A sign that the pineapple is ripe is if one of the inner leaves pulls out easily.

250g (9 oz) ripe pineapple, without skin
1 eating apple, weighing about 125g (4½ oz)
200g (7 oz) firm tofu
1 tbs agar-agar flakes
50ml (2 fl oz) water
100ml (4 fl oz) orange juice
1 egg white

Makes 6 small servings

Chop the pineapple, apple and tofu and blend in a liquidizer or food processor. Put to one side while you prepare the agar-agar which will make it set.

Heat the water and orange juice with the agar-agar flakes in a very small saucepan and let it simmer for 5 minutes stirring all the time. Take off the heat and add the agar-agar liquid to the blended fruit and tofu mixture.

Whisk the egg white stiffly and fold it into the fruit mixture. Pour into a bowl to set. An optional decoration is to sprinkle the top with a little cinnamon. Chill in the fridge before serving.

Each serving is 10g CHO. 50 kcals.

APRICOT MOUSSE

Dried apricots are so nutritious that they are often recommended in ordinary and special diets by dietitians. This is because of their high vitamin A content and because a portion of dried apricots contains more iron than the same weight of rump steak.

An unusual way to serve this mousse is to place peeled lychees around the sides of the serving dish.

175g (6 oz) dried apricots
300ml (11 fl oz) water
75g (3 oz) low-fat natural
    yogurt
150ml (5 fl oz) apple juice
50ml (2 fl oz) water
1 tbs agar-agar flakes
1 egg white

Makes 4 servings

Soak the apricots overnight in the 300ml (11 fl oz) water. Put the apricots and soaking water in a heavy saucepan and simmer gently until the water is absorbed, making sure that the apricots do not burn. Cool. Blend in a food processor or liquidizer to make a smooth cream. Fold in the yogurt.

Combine the apple juice, water and agar-agar flakes in a small saucepan and simmer for 5 minutes, stirring all the time. Stir the cooked agar-agar liquid into the apricot mixture. Whisk the egg white stiffly and fold in. Pour into 4 bowls and leave to set.

Each serving is 15g CHO. 70 kcals.

CAROB MOUSSE

200g (7 oz) firm tofu
200g (7 oz) ripe banana,
  peeled
½ tsp vanilla essence
4 tbs orange juice,
  unsweetened
1 tbs brandy (optional)
100g (4 oz) carob powder
200ml (7 fl oz) skimmed milk
200ml (7 fl oz) water
1 tbs agar-agar flakes or 2
  tsp agar-agar powder
2 egg whites

Makes 6 servings

Blend the tofu and banana in a food processor or food mill. Add the vanilla essence, orange juice and brandy and put to one side. In a small saucepan combine the carob powder, milk, water and agar-agar flakes. Bring to the boil and simmer on a low light for 5 minutes, stirring all the time and making sure the mixture does not become too thick.

If using agar-agar powder dissolve in 1 dessertspoon of water and add to the carob powder, milk and water in the saucepan after they have cooked gently for 3 minutes. Let the agar-agar solution simmer for a further 2 minutes.

Take the pan off the heat. Stir the agar-agar liquid into the tofu and banana mixture. Whisk the egg whites stiffly and fold in. Pour the mousse into 6 bowls and leave to set.

Each serving is 20g CHO. 100 kcals.

STRAWBERRY JELLY

The sweetness of this jelly is affected by the sweetness of the strawberries used. The English strawberries which appear in July and August seem to be sweeter than any of the imported ones on sale at other times of the year. When using those that do not have such a rich taste it is a good idea to include a few fresh dates or ripe banana for added flavour.

450g (1 lb) strawberries,
  hulled
100g (4 oz) fresh dates
  weighed with stones or
  100g (4 oz) ripe banana,
  peeled (optional)
150ml (5 fl oz) apple juice
50ml (2 fl oz) cold water
2 tsps agar-agar powder

Makes 4 servings

Blend the strawberries (and dates or banana) to make a bright pinky red purée. The small seeds on the outside of Spanish strawberries seem to be coarser than the English ones, so if you use this variety sieve the purée.

Combine the apple juice and water in a small saucepan. Use 1 tbs of this liquid to dissolve the agar-agar powder. Pour into the saucepan with the rest of the juice and water. Bring to the boil, add a little of the strawberry purée and simmer for 1½ minutes. Mix with the rest of the purée and pour into a wetted mould or bowls. The agar-agar powder sets very quickly. If you plan to pour the strawberry jelly into a mould have it ready beforehand so that it can be filled immediately after combining the agar-agar with the purée.

Each serving without added dates or banana is 10g CHO. 45 kcals.
Each serving with dates or banana is 15g CHO. 70 kcals.

Strawberry Jelly Ring: Fill the set jelly ring with strawberries and sliced kiwi fruit.

HONEYDEW JELLY

400g (14 oz) honeydew
  melon, without seeds
50g (2 oz) fresh dates, with
  stones
2 tsp agar-agar powder
100ml (4 fl oz) orange juice,
  unsweetened
100ml (4 fl oz) water
1 kiwi fruit for decoration

Makes 4 large servings

Scoop out the melon flesh from the rind and put in a blender with the sliced and stoned dates.

Mix the agar-agar powder with a little of the combined orange juice and water to make a thick paste then pour it into a small saucepan with the rest of the liquid and a little of the melon purée. Bring to the boil and continue to boil gently for 1½ minutes.

Combine with the rest of the melon and date purée and pour into glass bowls. (An alternative way of serving this jelly is to pour it into half the empty melon shell and use it as a large serving bowl.)

Decorate the jelly by placing slices of kiwi fruit on top. Chill before serving.

Each serving is 10g CHO. 45 kcals.

PEAR AND GRAPE JELLY

450g (1 lb) ripe pears, peeled
1½ tbs lemon juice, freshly squeezed
2 tsp agar-agar powder
100ml (4 fl oz) apple juice
50ml (2 fl oz) water
75g (3 oz) seedless grapes, halved, for decoration

Makes 4 servings

Cut the pears into chunks and blend with the lemon juice.

Mix the agar-agar powder with a little of the combined apple juice and water to make a thick paste. Add the rest of the liquid and pour into a saucepan with a little of the pear purée and boil for 1½–2 minutes. Add the agar-agar liquid to the remaining pear purée.

Pour into 4 serving glasses and decorate with halved grapes. Leave to set. Chill in the fridge before serving.

Each serving is 5g CHO. 70 kcals.

PINEAPPLE AND CHERRY JELLY

Using fruit juice is a quick way to prepare a jelly and I have included this recipe as an example of this method. It should be remembered that juice is a concentrated form of natural sugar, so for this reason chunks of whole fruit are introduced to provide some fibre and bulk to counteract the effects of the juice. Use the cartons of unsweetened pineapple juice that can be bought at most grocers.

300g (11 oz) fresh pineapple,
    without skin
100g (4 oz) cherries, stoned
1 tsp agar-agar powder
400ml (14 fl oz) pineapple
    juice

Makes 6 small servings

Before weighing the pineapple remove the skin. Make sure there are no remnants of the skin on the outside. Slice into bite-sized chunks. Slice the cherries in half. Put these two fruits on separate plates ready for use.

Mix the agar-agar powder with a little of the pineapple juice to make a thick paste. Gradually add more juice to make it into a runny liquid. Pour this together with any remaining juice into a medium-sized saucepan. Boil for 1½ minutes then pour immediately into a dampened mould.

Once the jelly is in the mould add the pineapple chunks then place the halved cherries around the outer edge of the mould. When the jelly has set and been removed from the mould, the edges around the base will be red. This has a particularly delicate effect with a fluted mould.

Each serving is 15g CHO. 65 kcals.

ORANGE CUPS

Oranges are associated with Mediterranean climates, but in fact originate from India. Nor are they naturally orange. In their native habitat they are often sold when the skin is green – yet they still taste just as sweet. Oranges are particularly high in vitamin C – 50mg per 100g – and because of this are recommended for people who have colds.

4 oranges weighing about
   600g (1lb 5 oz)
100ml (4 fl oz) apple juice
2 tsp agar-agar powder

**Makes 8 small or 4 large
   servings**

Cut the oranges in half. Remove the flesh carefully so as not to break the orange peel cups, and put them on a plate ready to be filled with the orange jelly.

Remove the pith and pips from the fruit. Blend the fruit and put it to one side in a bowl. Mix the agar-agar powder with a little of the apple juice. Pour this into a saucepan together with the rest of the juice and add a little of the blended orange. Bring to the boil and cook gently for 1½ minutes.

Take off the heat and add the agar-agar liquid to the rest of the puréed orange juice. Leave to stand until it cools a little then pour into the 8 orange halves.

Each orange half is 5g CHO. 25 kcals.

MANGO FOOL

This velvety dessert can be whizzed up in a matter of minutes. The mango originated in India and in recent years has become easier to obtain in Europe. Many different kinds of mangoes are grown, but only a few varieties are seen in the shops. Mostly they are either oval or kidney-shaped, about 10–15cm (4–6 in) long. They are usually yellow, with orange or red tinges in their skin when ready for eating, and give slightly to the touch when ripe. You can ripen a mango yourself at home by putting the fruit in a brown paper bag until ready. As soon as it is ripe, store in the fridge.

The one problem with mangoes is that they are amazingly messy to eat. The central stone is covered in hairs that cling on to the fibrous flesh around it and make it difficult to slice all the fruit off easily. It is a kindness on your part to prepare this fruit for your guests! The mango makes a superb fool and because it is a tropical fruit it is an unusual dessert.

Mangoes are high in carotene and vitamin C, although if the fruit is unripe it will not contain nearly as much carotene. It also contains small amounts of minerals.

2 large mangoes weighing about 550–600g (1lb 4oz- -1lb 6 oz)
1 tbs lemon juice, freshly squeezed
200ml (7 fl oz) Greek yogurt

Makes 6 servings

Peel the mango. Carefully slice the flesh around the stone into a bowl, making sure you do not lose any of the juice. Pour into the liquidizer with the lemon juice. Blend to make a purée.

Combine with the yogurt and spoon the fool into 6 bowls or glasses. Chill in the fridge before serving. Decorate with a few flaked almonds.

Each serving is 10g CHO. 80 kcals.

PINEAPPLE–TOFU CREAM

This is light, creamy and swiftly thrown together.

200g (7 oz) firm tofu
200g (7 oz) fresh pineapple, with the skin removed
75g (3 oz) ground almonds
cinnamon
almond flakes

Makes 4 servings

Blend or process the tofu and pineapple together. To achieve a really creamy texture you may need to put this mixture through a sieve or food mill. Add the ground almonds. Spoon into 4 bowls or glasses. Sprinkle lightly with cinnamon and a few almond flakes. Chill in the fridge before serving.

Each serving is 10g CHO. 160 kcals.

STRAWBERRY CREAM

'Doubtless God could have made a better berry, but doubtless God never did.'

> Dr William Butler (1536–1618), English physician regarded as 'the Aesculapius of our age'.

Strawberries taste so perfect it seems a shame to liquidize or purée them. Eat them with a little fromage frais and they are extra delicious. Fromage frais is a soft cheese produced from skimmed milk which tastes somewhere between yogurt and soft white cheese. It has a thick consistency and a creamy taste. There are two types available – a low fat version and a richer creamier one. The recipes in this book use the low-fat version which contains only 0.4 per cent fat – considerably less than the 21 per cent fat that single cream, the usual accompaniment to strawberries, contains. This means that fromage frais is lighter on the stomach and the conscience.

550g (1 lb 4 oz) strawberries, hulled
600g (1 lb 5 oz) fromage frais

Makes 4 servings

Combine the strawberries and fromage frais in a bowl. Leave to chill in the fridge for an hour. The cream will turn a little pink while standing. Serve chilled.

Each serving is 10g CHO. 105 kcals.

CRÈME AUX MARRONS

This quickly-made chestnut cream is versatile. It can serve as a cream dessert served in tall glasses or as a fancy filling for a swiss roll or cake.

50ml (2 fl oz) boiling water
50g (2 oz) dried apricots
200g (7 oz) chestnut purée, unsweetened
100ml (4 fl oz) skimmed milk
100g (4 oz) skimmed milk quark
1 tbs brandy

Makes 4 dessert servings

Pour the boiling water over the apricots and leave to stand for 15 minutes. Grind the apricots finely in an electric coffee grinder. Put them together with the chestnut purée and milk in a small saucepan. Cook over a very low heat and stir continuously until the milk has been absorbed and the whole mixture takes on a thick paste-like consistency.

Remove from the heat and add the quark and brandy. The cream is now a light honey-brown colour and ready for use.

As a dessert: spoon the cream into 4 glass bowls. Serve with a Cinnamon Hazelnut Stick (see page 000) in the middle of each dish.

As a cake filling: halve the ingredients. Spread the cream over the cake's surface. This quantity provides enough cream to cover the surface of a 22.5×30cm (9×12 in) swiss roll.

Each serving is 25g CHO. 145 kcals.

CAROB CREAM

This thick cream makes a delicious dessert.

2 tsp arrowroot
10g (¼ oz) carob powder
300ml (10 fl oz) skimmed milk
150g (5 oz) ripe banana, peeled
½ tsp vanilla essence

Makes 6 servings

Blend the arrowroot and carob powder in a small saucepan with enough milk to make a paste. Stir in the rest of the milk and slowly heat. Bring the mixture to the boil, stirring continuously. Cook for 3–4 minutes until the mixture thickens.

Take off the heat and add the finely mashed or sieved banana and the vanilla essence. Pour into glasses ready for serving. Leave in the fridge for a few hours to become firmer and chilled.

Each serving is 10g CHO. 45 kcals.

TRIFLE

Trifle, when you think about it, is nothing more than a combination of jelly, custard, fruit and cake. But, to take Alexander Pope's famous line from 'An Essay on Man' out of context, 'all are but parts of one stupendous whole'. Two versions of trifle are given here: one uses fruit that is available in the summer and the other uses fruit that is available in the winter.

½ quantity Swiss Roll (see page 147)

4 tbs orange juice (or 2 tbs orange juice and 2 tbs brandy)

Summer fruit trifle

2 small eating apples weighing 200g (7 oz)

250g (9 oz) cherries, with stones

200g (7 oz) peach

Jelly

3 oranges weighing about 550g (1 lb 4 oz) with skin

scant 2 tsp agar-agar powder

100ml (4 fl oz) apple juice

2 quantities Banana Custard (see page 159)

Topping

300g (11 oz) strawberries, hulled

300ml (11 fl oz) fromage frais

Bake the swiss roll sponge. Half will be used in this recipe and half can be frozen for future use. Cut the sponge into small bite-sized pieces and lay around the base of an attractive serving bowl. Pour the orange juice or juice and brandy over the top. Chop the apples and spread them evenly over the sponge. Chop the cherries and spread these over the apple. Chop the peach and spread thinly over the cherry layer.

Prepare the jelly: peel the oranges and remove any pith or seeds. Blend in the liquidizer to make 400ml (14 fl oz) liquid. Mix the agar-agar powder with the apple juice and pour into a small saucepan. Add a little of the blended orange pulp. Bring to the boil. Add the rest of the orange pulp and simmer for 1½–2 minutes. Pour over the fruit and sponge. This will hold it in place.

Prepare the Banana Custard and pour over the jelly, which will have set quite quickly.

Prepare the topping: combine the sliced strawberries with the fromage frais and spread over the top of the custard, which should be fairly firm. Leave to chill in the fridge for a couple of hours before serving. The trifle still tastes very good, some say even better, after a night in the fridge.

Follow the instructions for the summer trifle but substitute the different fruit where appropriate.

Each portion is 25g CHO. 200 kcals.

Winter fruit version
2 small eating apples
    weighing 200g (7 oz)
5 kiwi fruit
150g (5 oz) seedless grapes,
    halved

Jelly
3 oranges weighing about
    550g (1 lb 4 oz) with skin
100ml (4 fl oz) apple juice
scant 2 tsp agar-agar powder

2 quantities Banana Custard
    (see page 159)

Topping
200g (7 oz) mango
300ml (11 oz) fromage frais

Makes 8 large servings

BANANA VELVET ICE CREAM

This ice cream is as soft as the kind that comes flowing out of commercial vending machines – the only difference is that the ingredients are all natural. It can either be served as soon as it is made or prepared a couple of hours before it is needed and stored in a covered container in the bottom of the freezer – this gives it a thicker and firmer texture.

The secret of this recipe lies in its use of frozen bananas. If bananas are particularly cheap one week I buy extra and freeze them in quantities of 200g (7 oz) in freezer bags so that they are on hand for the arrival of unexpected hot weather.

200g (7 oz) bananas, peeled
150ml (5 fl oz) low-fat
    natural yogurt

Makes 4 servings

Cut the bananas into thin slices, place them in a freezer bag and freeze until they are hard.

Use the sharp blade of a food processor. Place the frozen banana pieces and yogurt in the food processor and pulse gently, switching it on and off for short bursts. At the beginning the machine responds jerkily to the frozen banana, but after a while this is converted into a rich cream.

Each serving is 10g CHO. 60 kcals.

MELON AND RASPBERRY ICE CREAM

The fragrant galia melon blends well with raspberries in this scrumptious pink-coloured ice cream. It is not as sweet as Banana Velvet Ice Cream. If you need extra sweetness scatter a few chopped sultanas across the top.

600g (1 lb 5 oz) ripe galia melon
175g (6 oz) raspberries, frozen
150ml (5 fl oz) low-fat natural yogurt

Makes 6 servings

Cut the melon off the rind and discard the seeds. Slice the melon into chunks and freeze in a freezer bag until they become hard.

Use the sharp blade of a food processor. Place the frozen melon and raspberries with the yogurt in the food processor and pulse gently, switching it on and off for short bursts until the fruit becomes creamy.

Each serving is 5g CHO. 35 kcals.

Serving suggestion: the thick creamy texture of this ice cream makes it suitable for pouring onto a sweet pastry base to make a delicious ice cream tart.

ALMOND CAROB ICE CREAM

The advantage of this recipe is that the ice cream keeps its thick creamy form and can be kept in the fridge for a few hours until needed. It also works well as an unusual filling for pastry or plain cakes, such as Ice Cream Torte (see page 105–6). The hint of carob in this recipe colours the ice cream a pale brown, but does not overload the taste-buds.

Because frozen banana is used you will need to use a food processor to blend it to a cream.

150g (5 oz) firm tofu
200g (7 oz) banana, sliced
  and frozen
15g (½ oz) carob powder
few drops of almond essence

Makes 4 generous servings

Use the sharp cutting blade of a food processor. Put all the ingredients in the food processor and pulse gently, switching it on and off for short bursts for as long as is necessary until the ingredients form a thick cream. Store in the fridge until needed.

Each serving is 15g CHO. 70 kcals.

STRAWBERRY ICE

This very fruity ice can be made with either yogurt or, if you prefer, with tofu for a milk-free version.

400g (14 oz) strawberries,
  hulled
4 tbs apple juice,
  unsweetened
100g (4 oz) banana, peeled
100ml (4 fl oz) low-fat yogurt
  or 100g (4 oz) firm tofu

Makes 4 large servings

Blend the strawberries in a liquidizer with the apple juice. Add the banana and yogurt or firm tofu and blend to make a creamy liquid.

Pour the mixture into a freezer container. Cover with the lid and freeze for about 1–1½ hours until the sides of the ice cream have become frozen. Take it out of the freezer and blend again, beating air into it. Pour back into the container and return to the freezer for a further 2 hours or until needed. Put in the fridge 45 minutes before serving to thaw slightly.

Each serving is 15g CHO. 65 kcals.

PEACH ICE CREAM

For a really special dessert serve this ice cream with hot peach sauce (see page 156–7). This recipe uses the skin of the peaches to keep the fibre content high.

400g (14 oz) peaches
100g (4 oz) fresh dates, with stones
1 tbs lemon juice
1 tbs apple juice
100ml (4 fl oz) low-fat natural yogurt

Makes 4 servings

Chop the peaches into a blender. Stone the dates and blend with the juices.

Add the yogurt and blend for a few seconds.

Pour the ice cream mixture into a freezer container. Cover with the lid and freeze for about 1 hour until the sides are just beginning to set. Take the ice cream out of the freezer and blend again, beating air into it. Pour back into the container and return to the freezer for a further 2 hours or until needed. Put in the fridge 45 minutes before serving to thaw slightly.

Each serving is 15g CHO. 70 kcals.

MANGO CHERRY ICE CREAM

A delicious fruit ice cream that is quick to make and ideal for those on a milk-free diet.

1 mango weighing about 300–325g (11–11½ oz)
100g (4 oz) firm tofu
3 tbs apple juice, unsweetened
50g (2 oz) dark red cherries

Makes 4 medium-sized servings

Peel the mango and slice the fruit away from the inner stone. Put in a blender with the tofu and apple juice. Blend until a thick creamy purée is formed. Pour into a freezer container. Chop the cherries and stir them in so that they are well distributed in the ice cream. Cover with the lid and freeze until almost ready to serve. Place in the fridge 30–45 minutes before serving to thaw slightly.

Alternatively leave in the freezer for 2½–3 hours and serve before the ice cream is frozen solid.

Each scoop is 10g CHO. 55 kcals.

OAT ICE CREAM

The custard base of this ice cream gives it a creamy richness.

50g (2 oz) porridge oats
2 egg yolks
1 tsp arrowroot
150ml (5 fl oz) skimmed milk
150ml (5 fl oz7 low-fat
   fromage frais
100g (4 oz) banana, peeled

Makes 6 servings

Pour the oats onto a shallow ovenproof dish and bake in a preheated oven gas mark 4/180°C/350°F for 15 minutes or until lightly browned.

Combine the egg yolks and arrowroot in a bowl. Put the milk in a small saucepan and bring almost to the boil. Take it off the heat and slowly pour over the yolks, mixing them together. Pour this mixture back into the pan and stir with a wooden spoon until the mixture has thickened enough to coat the back of the spoon. (For tips on making custard, see page 158.)

Pour the custard into a bowl and add the fromage frais and the sieved or moulied banana. Fold in the roasted oats and leave to cool for 15 minutes before freezing. Place in a freezer container, cover with the lid and freeze until thick (about 2 hours).

Each serving is 10g CHO. 100 kcals.

FROZEN STRAWBERRY SUNDAES

Liqueur-flavoured strawberry ice cream sitting in a frozen strawberry case decorated with a lustrous green grape makes a colourful and unusual dessert.

350g (12 oz) large
   strawberries, hulled
90–100g (3½–4 oz) hulled
   strawberries
1 tbs apple juice
1 tbs calvados
25g (1 oz) banana, peeled
25g (1 oz) firm tofu
small green seedless grapes

Makes 4 servings

Prepare the strawberry cases: hollow out the 350g (12 oz) large strawberries, leaving their outer shells quite thick. Before doing this observe which way they sit because when served they should stand upright. It might be more practical to hollow out some of the strawberries slightly off-centre.

Prepare the ice cream: combine the insides of the strawberries with the 90–100g (3½–4 oz) quantity to make up a total weight of 100g (4 oz) strawberries. Blend with the apple juice, calvados, banana and tofu. Stand this fruit purée in a shallow dish in the freezer for about 30 minutes or until it has begun to set around the sides and has become thick and creamy.

Place the large hollowed-out strawberries in a shallow freezer container. Spoon the fruit ice into each strawberry. If it is thick enough pile it up on top, but avoid it running down the sides and coating the outside of the strawberry.

Return to the freezer for about 30 minutes then remove and place one small grape on the top of each strawberry. Cover and return to the bottom of the freezer, where the strawberries will freeze more slowly and after a few hours the ice will be set but the fruit will not be rock hard. If you prepare this dessert the day before, remove the sundaes from the freezer to the fridge 30 minutes before serving.

Each serving is 10g CHO. 45 kcals.

FRUIT ICE LOLLIES

Fresh fruit can be frozen to make quite delicious ices. Use either the whole fruit or slices of fruit and freeze until solid. This is an even simpler method than mixing juice and water and pouring it into a mould, and the fruit lollies are such a novelty that they are an instant success with everyone.

When choosing fruit for freezing always use fruit that is fresh and not bruised or over-ripe for the best results. Very sweet fruits are ideal since the sweet flavour usually diminishes during freezing.

The carbohydrate and calorie value of the individual lollies is very low and because they are frozen they take longer to eat.

Strawberry Ice Lollies
These are very simple to make and popular with everyone. Use fresh beautifully rounded strawberries in season. Hull and wash the fruit. Cut a brightly coloured plastic straw in half or insert a wooden cocktail stick in the centre of each strawberry. Place the strawberries in a container, putting greaseproof paper between the layers, and freeze until hard (this will vary with size – a few hours at most).

Freezing changes the texture of the strawberry, but it does not affect its bright colour.

150g (5 oz) strawberries is 10g CHO. 40 kcals.

Melon Ice
Honeydew or galia melons freeze well. Remove the seeds and rind and cut the melon into chunks. Lay them out on a freezer tray, making sure that they are not touching, and freeze until hard.

Red watermelon looks very attractive when frozen and makes a very icy mouthful because of its high water content, but it is fiddly work removing all the seeds.

200g (7 oz) melon without the rind is 10g CHO. 40 kcals.

Peach Ice Pops
Peaches have a firm texture and freeze well. Cut thick slices and spear them with a cocktail stick through the middle then freeze.

100g (4 oz) peaches is 10g CHO. 40 kcals.

Iced Fruit Kebab
For this unusual end to a meal, use wooden skewers. Put 3 seedless grapes at each end of the skewers and alternate 2 whole strawberries with 2 slices of peach, 2 slices of honeydew melon and 2 thin slices of banana, then freeze.

12 CHILDREN'S PARTIES

Ices, lollies, jellies, biscuits and cakes – the traditional ingredients of a children's party – can all be found in the pages of this book.

The sweet treats that children enjoy most at a party are ices and lollies. Biscuits and cakes are never in great demand. They are visually appealing, but it is usually parents who eat them rather than children. It is the savoury foods that are always the most popular – crisps, fish fingers, and pizzas and quiches for older children. Sandwiches have a solid minority appeal. Titbits such as salted popcorn, raisins and their carob-coated cousins also go down well.

A midday party shifts the emphasis even more towards savoury foods. Fish fingers or coated chicken served with chips, crisps or potatoes in their jackets are top favourites. Follow them up with Strawberry Ice Lollies or ice cream and all will be content. The pleasurable side of lunch parties is that the guests are hungry and eat most of the food, unlike tea where they tend to take one bite and move on to the next delicacy.

Popular party recipes which are simple to make are:

– *Strawberry Ice Lollies* (see page 179). These are always a huge success. Even children who usually eat strawberries doused in sugar ask for seconds.

– *Banana Velvet Ice Cream* (see page 173–4). Prepare this a couple of hours beforehand and store it in the bottom of the freezer so that when it is needed it will be firm but not frozen solid. If there are not too many guests, sprinkle the round scoops of ice cream with desiccated coconut and use carob-coated raisins for eyes.

– *Strawberry Jelly* (see page 164–5).

– *Apricot Fairy Cakes* (see page 150–51). Bake these in petits fours cases and decorate with a blob of coloured coconut icing in the centre.

– *Jam Tarts*. Use one of the simple pastry recipes (see page 86–92). Cut the pastry into circles, place in a jam tart tray, fill with sugar-free jam and bake in a quick oven.

– *Carob Almond Balls* (see page 65).

– *Cinnamon Drops* (see page 66–7).

– *Carob Secrets* (see page 66). Serve these in miniature paper cases.

– *Marzipan Mice* (see page 72–3).

The Birthday Cake

Banana Cake (see page 135), Apple Cherry Cake (see page 134) or Carrot Cake (see page 141) make a scrumptious base with a texture that is firm enough to be cut into shapes. Swiss Roll (see page 147–8) filled with sugar-free jam is excellent for any design that requires a cylindrical shape, and is popular with children.

Decorating birthday cakes
There are five toppings you can use for decorating a birthday cake:

– *Carob Icing* (see page 56).

– *Coconut Icing* (see page 57).

– spreading the cake's surface with sugar-free jam and sprinkling *desiccated coconut* all over. The coconut can be used as it is or coloured.

– sprinkling *carob flakes* over the cream surface of a cake. Make them by melting a good quality carob bar (see Carob Apricot Treats page 71). Spread the carob thinly over a sheet of greaseproof paper. After a few minutes cut long thin lines across the surface and when you remove it from the paper, the carob will break into thin flakes.

– *quark* or *fromage frais* can be coloured and used to cover the surface of the cake. By itself it is not particularly sweet and you will find that the addition of a little puréed dried apricot or puréed banana with a drop of lemon juice to avoid discolouring makes a considerable difference to the taste.
To emphasize details on the cake choose either:

– *Fresh fruit*, particularly the bright ones such as kiwi fruit, strawberries, oranges and green grapes. They look very effective but need to be prepared on the day of the party because they will not look so fresh and bright if prepared earlier.

– *Dried fruit:* raisins, sultanas, slivers of prune, dried apricots and long strips of dried banana, circles of dried pear or peach can all be used to enhance letters or a design.

– *Marzipan:* this can be used for lettering, railway lines or trimming around the edge of a cake. The sugar-free version will not take as much detail as marzipan made with sugar so avoid a design that requires dense detail.

Colouring
Colouring that uses natural ingredients is available in the shops. If you prefer to make your own try raspberry concentrate or the juice of fresh blackberries for pink, turmeric or carrot juice for yellow, cinnamon for light brown.

Simple ideas for cakes
There is an infinite number of designs that you can make using the five basic icings.

Happy Birthday Cake: This is very quick to decorate. Cover the cake either in carob icing or sugar-free jam with tinted desiccated coconut sprinkled over the top. Pipe the child's name or 'happy birthday' in plain white quark which can be flavoured with a few drops of vanilla essence. Decorate the sides with halved strawberries or kiwi fruit slices.

Name Cakes: Alphabet letters made of cake provide a strong visual effect.
    Bake a double quantity of cake in a rectangular tin about 30×20cm (12×8 in). Cut in half lengthways. Use one half to cut into equal lengths – these will provide the straight part of such letters as l, t, h, d, b, k, and rounded shapes such as a, o, u, c (see diagram on page 184). One way of making this easier is to place a toy letter in front of you while cutting it out or to draw it on a piece of greaseproof paper, cut it out and place it on the cake as you cut around it.
    Cover a large tray with silver foil on which to assemble the letters needed to write the child's name. Jam is a useful glue for sticking together the different sections of the letters. Coat with carob icing and sprinkle with desiccated coconut.
    If you have leftover cake an extra touch that goes down well is to use a gingerbread cutter to make a boy or girl and decorate them, adding a few fruit details for eyes, hands and feet.

Train Cake: An old favourite. Bake two swiss rolls about 30×20cm (12×8 in). Roll one up, spreading the inside with jam. This will be the basis for the engine.

Cut the remaining swiss roll into five strips crossways, each one about 5cm (2 in) wide. Place one of these under the completed swiss roll so that it will have the same width as the railway wagons. Cut the remaining strips in half so that each one is about 10×5cm (4×2 in). Build these up to make three low wagons.

Cover the engine in carob icing. Use coloured skimmed milk quark for the wagons. Most children will not enjoy quark by itself. A simple sweetener is to add 25g (1 oz) ground dried apricots per 100g (4 oz) quark or 50g (2 oz) puréed banana with a few drops of lemon juice. Colour each wagon a bright colour – yellow, green and pink go well together.

Cover a large tray with silver foil to assemble the train on. For railway tracks use either coloured straws or strips of dried banana. Place the engine and its wagons on the railway lines. Use slices of banana dipped in lemon juice as wheels and a thicker piece to sit on top of the engine as the funnel. Use strips of dried apricot to connect the engine and wagons together. Pile the wagons high with coloured cargo such as strawberries or cherries. Decorate the window of the engine with pieces of dried apple. A small engine driver or guard can be placed on the appropriate part of the train.

Cat's Face: The central part of the cat's face is built up to give a three-dimensional effect. This makes a much greater impact than a flat one-

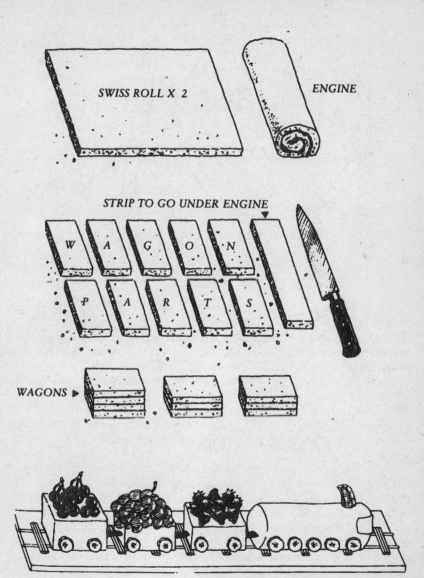

SWISS ROLL X 2

ENGINE

STRIP TO GO UNDER ENGINE

W A G O N

P A R T S

WAGONS ▶

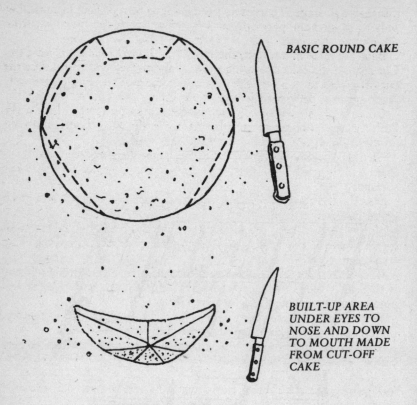

BASIC ROUND CAKE

*BUILT-UP AREA
UNDER EYES TO
NOSE AND DOWN
TO MOUTH MADE
FROM CUT-OFF
CAKE*

dimensional shape. There is no need for it to be a perfect likeness, but only to suggest the part of a cat's face that protrudes the most, from the eyes to the nose.

Bake the cake in a round, shallow 22.5–30cm (9–12 in) baking tin. Cut around the cake according to the diagram (see page 300). Use the cut-off pieces to build up the area under the eyes. It should gradually reach up to a peak for the nose then rapidly descend to the mouth.

Cover the cake with a double quantity of carob icing. Because the built-up area will have an irregular surface let the icing harden and pour an extra batch on top to give a smoother finish.

The facial details bring the cat to life so use brightly coloured fruit. Place a little icing underneath the fruit to set it firmly on the cake's surface:

– *Eyes* slanted slices of peach or orange segments with a seedless green grape propped up against the middle for a pupil.

– *Nose* – place a blob of quark or Greek yogurt on the highest point for the base of the nose. Use either a cherry or the round end of a strawberry for the nose.

– *Whiskers* – take 4 large dried apricots and cut them round and round with a sharp knife to make long curly strips. Gently unfurl them and place two on each side of the nose.

– *Mouth* – at the base of the built-up section, directly under the nose, place a round piece of plum with the skin side showing.

– *Ears* – spread the inside of the ears with a little quark or Greek yogurt. Either leave them white or tint a pale pink.

If the carbohydrate or calorie count has to be watched remember to add on the value of the icing and the dried or fresh fruit.

Natural Sugar and Fibre in Food

(n/a = not available, tr = trace, neg = negligible)

100g	fibre	natural sugars	calories
Almonds, shelled	14.3g	4.3g	565
Apple, eating	1.5g	9.1g	35
Apple juice, unsweetened	neg	12.0g	45
Apricots, dried	24.0g	43.4g	182
Apricots, fresh	1.9g	6.2g	25
Apricots, hunza	21.2g	38.3g	160
Arrowroot	n/a	tr	355
Banana, peeled	3.4g	16.2g	79
Banana, dried	9.4g	53.0g	210
Barley flakes	6.0g	n/a	315
Barley flour	2.4g	n/a	360
Beans, aduki, raw	9.0g	n/a	280
Bran, wheat	44.0g	3.8g	180
Brazil nuts, shelled	9.0g	1.7g	619
Butter	0g	0g	740
Carob powder	55.2g	n/a	200
Carrots, raw	2.9g	5.4g	25
Cherries, fresh whole	1.5g	10.4g	40
Chestnut purée	6.8g	7.0g	170
Chicory	n/a	n/a	9
Clementine	1.3g	8.0g	23
Coconut cream	n/a	n/a	330
Coconut, desiccated	23.5g	6.4g	604

100g	fibre	natural sugars	calories
Dates, dried, stoned	8.7g	63.9g	248
Dates, fresh	n/a	18.0g	80
Eggs	0g	0g	145
Figs, dried raw	18.5g	52.9g	213
Figs, fresh	2.5g	9.5g	41
Flour, brown rice	8.0g	n/a	310
Flour, soya	15.0g	13.5g	375
Flour, wholewheat	9.6g	2.3g	318
Fromage frais, low-fat	0g	n/a	50
Gooseberries	3.2g	3.4g	17
Grapes, green seedless	0.9g	16.1g	63
Hazelnuts without shells	6.1g	4.7g	380
Jam, sugar-free	5.6g	34.0g	120
Kiwi fruit	n/a	7.0g	35
Lemon, whole	5.2g	3.2g	15
Lemon juice	0g	1.6g	7
Mango	1.5g	15.3g	59
Margarine, polyunsaturated	0g	0.1g	730
Melon, honeydew with skin	0.6g	3.1g	13
Melon, watermelon with skin	n/a	2.7g	11
Milk, skimmed	0g	5.0g	33
Millet	5.0g	n/a	380
Millet flakes	5.0g	n/a	380
Oats, porridge	7.0g	tr	401
Oat bran with germ	18.0g	n/a	420
Oil (sunflower, soya bean, olive oil, sesame seed)	0g	0g	900
Orange, with peel	1.5g	6.4g	26
Orange juice	0g	9.4g	38
Parsnip, cooked	4.0g	8.8g	56
Passion fruit with skin	6.7g	2.6g	14
Peach with stone	1.2g	7.9g	32

100g	fibre	natural sugars	calories
Peanut butter	7.6g	6.7g	630
Peanuts, without shells	8.1g	3.1g	570
Pears, fresh	2.3g	10.6g	41
Pecan nuts	5.0g	n/a	680
Pineapple, fresh	1.2g	11.6g	46
Pine nuts	4.0g	n/a	580
Poppy seeds	n/a	n/a	560
Prunes, dried, stoned	16.1g	40.3g	161
Pumpkin seeds	n/a	n/a	555
Pomegranate	n/a	9.1g	35
Quark, skimmed milk	0g	n/a	80
Raisins	6.8g	64.4g	246
Raspberries	7.4g	5.6g	25
Redcurrants	8.2g	4.4g	21
Rhubarb, raw	2.6g	1.0g	6
Rice, brown, raw	4.2g	n/a	360
Rice flakes, brown	4.2g	n/a	360
Rosewater	neg	neg	neg
Rye flakes	6.0g	n/a	315
Rye flour	n/a	tr	335
Satsuma	1.9g	8.0g	35
Sesame seeds	3.9g	n/a	500
Shredded wheat, 1 biscuit	3.3g	neg	80
Soya bean flakes	15.0g	n/a	385
Soya milk	0g	n/a	60
Strawberries, fresh	2.2g	6.2g	26
Sultanas	7.0g	64.7g	250
Sunflower seeds	3.6g	n/a	560
Tahini	5.2g	n/a	600
Tofu, firm	0g	n/a	70
Tomatoes, raw	1.5g	2.8g	14
Walnuts, shelled	5.2g	3.2g	525
Wheat flakes	12.3g	0.4g	325
Wheatgerm	n/a	16.0g	345
Wholewheat noodles	11.0g	n/a	340

100g	fibre	natural sugars	calories
Yeast, baker's	6.9g	tr	53
Yogurt, Greek	0g	4.0g	135
Yogurt, low-fat natural	0g	6.2g	52

INDEX

Aduki and apple pie 94
Agar-agar 160
Almond
    and banana roll 106
    and pine crescents 67
    apricot spread 53
    carob balls 65
    carob ice cream 174
    frutti tart 104
    globes, chilled, in pastel pink
        sauce 117
    pastry 90
    pudding 122
Apple(s)
    and aduki pie 94
    and pear pie with crumble
        topping 93
    and pineapple mousse 162
    and poppy seed cake 137
    and wheatgerm 29
    baked 130
    cherry cake 134
    crumble 125
    custard 121
    fibre content 22
    meringue 121
    rice pudding 125
    slice 134
    stewed 128
    strudel 96
Apricot(s)
    almond spread 53
    carob treats 71
    dried, fibre content 22

fairy cakes 150
mousse 163
ring 111
sponge pudding 124
tart 103
wild Himalayan, in rosewater 116
Artificial sweeteners 7–8
Ascorbic acid (Vitamin C) 9, 35
Aspartame 7–8

Baby foods 6
Bagels 39
Baked
    apples 130
    bananas 130
Banana(s)
    and almond roll 106
    baked 130
    cake 135
    custard 159
    fibre content 22
    tahini spread 54
    velvet ice cream 173
Barley
    loaf 47
    pastry 90
Biscuits 5
Bread
    basic method of making 34
    brown 21
    kneading 35–6
    rolls 35
        without Vitamin C 37
    Rye 38

Breakfast cereals 5
British Dental Association 15
British Federation of Bakers 33
British Medical Association 16
British Nutritional Foundation
    (BNF) 16
Butter, peanut 6, 52

Cake(s)
  apple cherry 134
  apple slice 134
  apricot fairy 150
  banana 135
  birthday 182
  carob 139
  carob mousse layer 140
  carrot 141
  fruit 153
  parsnip 142
  pineapple tang 136
  poppy seed and apple 137
  Swiss roll 147, 149
  walnut 152
Cancer of the large bowel 18
Canderel 7
Carob
  almond balls 65
  almond ice cream 174
  apricot treats 71
  cake 139
  cream 171
  cream tart 102
  fudge squares 62
  hazelnut cream filling 55
  hazelnut slice 64
  icing 56
  mousse 164
  mousse layer cake 140
  orange pie 98
  roll 107
  secrets 66
  swiss roll 149
Carrot(s)
  and orange soup 30
  cake 141
  fibre content 22
  peanut salad 77

Cheesecake
  cherry 143
  persimmon 145
  tofu apple 146
  yeast 144
Cherry
  and pineapple jelly 167
  apple cake 134
  cheesecake 143
  compôte 129
  cream 55
  mango ice cream 176
  sauce 155
Chestnut
  and satsuma cream filling 56
  crème aux marrons 170
  fudge fingers 60
Chicory salad 78
Children's parties
  birthday cakes 182
  treats for 181
Chilled almond globes in pastel pink
    sauce 117
Chinese cabbage and orange salad 78
Chocolate 4
Chutney(s)
  French-Canadian 80
  mango 82
  pineapple date 80
Cinnamon
  drops 66
  hazelnut sticks 69
  roll 110
Clementine cream delight 112
Coconut
  icing 57
Compôte, cherry 129
Confectionery 3
Conserve, pineapple 54
Consumption of sugar, figures 3–4
Coronary Prevention Group 16
Cream(s)
  carob 171
  cherry 55
  pineapple-tofu 169
  strawberry 170
Crème aux marrons 170

Crohn's disease 18
Crumble(s)
  apple 125
Custard 158
  apple 121
  banana 159

Date(s)
  delight 113
  dried, fibre content 22
  pineapple chutney 80
DDT 11
Dextrose 3
Diabetes, diabetics 17
Diarrhoea 8, 18
Diverticular disease 18
Dough, kneading 35–6
Doughnuts 42
Dressings
  French or vinaigrette 76
  Mediterranean 77
  oil used in 75
Dried fruit 6
  minerals in 9
Drop scones 48

Fairy cakes, apricot 150
Fibre 21–23
  and natural sugar content in
    food 187
  content in food 22
Fig(s)
  au fromage frais 114
  dried, fibre content 22
Food, natural sugar and fibre content
  in 187
Fool(s)
  mango 168
Freezing 23
French-Canadian chutney 80
French dressing (vinaigrette) 76
Fresh fruit, as sweeteners 6–7
Fromage frais, figs au 114
Frozen strawberry sundaes 178
Fructose 3
Fruit
  bars 4

cake 153
how to dry 9–10
ice lollies 179
juice 6
loaf 41
salad, July 115
stewed 126
tarts 101
tinned in natural juice 6
yogurt 5, 29
Frutti almond tart 104
Fudge
  carob squares 62
  chestnut fingers 60
  pecan 70

Gallstones 18
  fibre content 22
  syrup 3
Grape(s)
  and pear jelly 166
  Iced, in A Flaming Pink Sea 119

Hasty pastry 86
Hazelnut(s)
  carob cream filling 55
  carob slice 64
  cinnamon sticks 69
  pastry 91
Heart disease 16
High blood pressure 16
Honey 8
  fibre content 22
Honeydew jelly 165
Hypoglycaemia 18

Ice cream
  almond carob 174
  banana velvet 173
  mango cherry 176
  melon and raspberry 174
  oat 177
  peach 176
  torte 105
Ice lollies, fruit 179
Iced Grapes in a Flaming Pink
  Sea 119

Icings
  carob 56
  coconut 57
Ingredients, basic 24–6
Invert syrup 3

Jelly
  honeydew 165
  pear and grape 166
  pineapple and cherry 167
  strawberry 164
July fruit salad 115

Lemon
  scones 46
Loaf,
  barley 47
  fruit 41
Lucozade 4

Maimonides 19
Mango
  cherry ice cream 176
  chutney 82
  fool 168
  pie delight 95
Marrons, crème aux 170
Marzipan 71
  fruit 72
  mice 72
Mayonnaise 75
  sugar-free 5
Measurements 24
Mediterranean dressing 77
Mediterranean half moons 58
Melon
  and raspberry ice cream 174
  bowls 115
  ice 179
Meringue, apple 121
Migraine, theobromine 62
Millet peach delight 118
Minerals,
  in dried fruit 9
Mood and behaviour 19
Mousse
  apricot 163

carob 164
pineapple and apple 162
strawberry 161
Muesli 28

National Advisory Committee on
    Nutrition Education
    (NACNE) 74
National Commission on Diabetes 17
Natural sugar and fibre content in
    food 187
Noodle pudding 123
NutraSweet 7

Oat(s)
  ice cream 177
  sesame bars 61
  snacks 61
Oatcakes 50
Obesity 16
Oils used in dressings 75
Orange
  and carrot soup 30
  and Chinese cabbage salad 78
  and strawberry sauce 155
  carob pie 98
  cups 168
  fritters 119
Organic food 12–13

Parsnip cake 142
Pastel pink sauce 156
Pastry
  almond 90
  barley 90
  hasty 86
  hazelnut 91
  rough puff 88
  short cut strudel 87
  sweet seed 91
  yeast 92
  yogurt 86
Peach(es)
  custard tart 99
  ice cream 176
  ice pops 179
  millet delight 118

poached 128
sauce 156
Peanut(s)
    butter 6, 52
    carrot salad 77
    scones 45
Pear(s)
    and apple pie with crumble
        topping 93
    and grape jelly 166
    and prune drops 68
    and spiced melon 82
    stewed 127
Pecan
    fudge 70
    pie 97
Persimmon cheesecake 145
Pesticides, effects on food 11–12
Phenylketonura 8
Phenylalanine 8
Pies
    apple and pear with crumble
        topping 93
    mango delight 95
    orange carob 98
    pecan 97
Pine and almond crescents 67
Pineapple
    and apple mousse 162
    and cherry jelly 167
    conserve 54
    date chutney 80
    tang cake 136
    tofu cream 169
Poached peaches 128
Pomegranate dip 113
Poppy seed
    and apple cake 137
    torte 151
Prune(s)
    and pear drops 68
    fibre content 22
Pudding
    almond 122
    apple rice 125
    apricot sponge 124
    noodle 123

summer 30

Raisin(s)
    fibre content 22
Raspberry(ies)
    and melon ice cream 174
    sauce 157
Ribena 4
Rice
    apple pudding 125
Roll(s)
    banana and almond 106
    bread 35
    without Vitamin C 37
carob 107
cinnamon 110
Rough Puff Pastry 88
Royal Bristol Infirmary 18
Royal College of Physicians 16, 18
Rye bread 38

Saccharin 7
Salads
    chicory 77
    orange and chinese cabbage 78
    peanut carrot 77
Satsuma chestnut cream filling 56
Sauces
    cherry 155
    orange and strawberry 155
    pastel pink 117, 156
    peach 156
    raspberry 157
Scones 44
    drop 48
    lemon 46
    peanut45
Sesame
    oat bars 61
    squares 59
Short cut strudel 87
Singin' Hinny 50
Soft drinks 4
Sorbitol 8
Soup, orange and carrot 30
Spiced melon and pears 82
Spots and pimples 18

Spreads
  apricot almond 53
  tahini-banana 54
Stewed
  apple 28
  fruit 126
  pears 127
Storing dried fruit, nuts and
  grains 10–11
Strawberry
  and orange sauce 155
  cream 170
  hats 109
  ice 175
  ice lollies 179
  jelly 164
  mousse 161
  sundaes, frozen 178
  tart 100
Strudel
  apple 96
  short cut 87
Substitutes 22–3
Sucrose 3
Sugar
  and your health 14–19
  fibre content 22
  how to shake off 2
  spot the 2–3
Sugar Bureau 15
Sugar-free shopping 3–6
Sultanas
  fibre content 22
Summer pudding 30
Sunflower chews 70
Sweet
  seed pastry 91
Sweeteners 6–7
  dried fruit 6
  fresh fruit 6–7
  juice 7
Swiss roll 147

carob 149

Tahini-banana spread 54
Tarts
  apricot 103
  carob cream 102
  fruit 101
  frutti almond 104
  melon and raspberry ice cream 174
  peach custard 99
  strawberry 100
  Theobromine and migraine 62
Tofu
  apple cheesecake 146
Tooth decay 15
Torte
  ice cream 105
  poppy seed 151
Trifle 172

UK Registry for Organic Food
  Standards 13
USA Food and Drug
  Administration 7

Vinaigrette (French dressing) 76
Vitamin C (ascorbic acid) 9, 35

Walnut
  cake 152
  crescents 108
Wheatgerm and apple 29
Wild Himalayan apricots in
  rosewater 116

Yeast
  cheesecake 144
  pastry 92
Yogurt
  fruit 5, 29
  pastry 86